The EDUCATION of BRAINIAC

A New Yorker's Quest for the Good Life in the Hub of the Universe

DAVID E. LAPIN

To Richard, with much appreciation for being part of Brainiac's story,

David
11-20-19

iUniverse

THE EDUCATION OF BRAINIAC
A NEW YORKER'S QUEST FOR THE GOOD
LIFE IN THE HUB OF THE UNIVERSE

Copyright © 2019 David E. Lapin.

All rights reserved. No part of this book may be used or reproduced by any means, graphic, electronic, or mechanical, including photocopying, recording, taping or by any information storage retrieval system without the written permission of the author except in the case of brief quotations embodied in critical articles and reviews.

iUniverse books may be ordered through booksellers or by contacting:

iUniverse
1663 Liberty Drive
Bloomington, IN 47403
www.iuniverse.com
1-800-Authors (1-800-288-4677)

Because of the dynamic nature of the Internet, any web addresses or links contained in this book may have changed since publication and may no longer be valid. The views expressed in this work are solely those of the author and do not necessarily reflect the views of the publisher, and the publisher hereby disclaims any responsibility for them.

Any people depicted in stock imagery provided by Getty Images are models, and such images are being used for illustrative purposes only. Certain stock imagery © Getty Images.

ISBN: 978-1-5320-8063-0 (sc)
ISBN: 978-1-5320-8065-4 (hc)
ISBN: 978-1-5320-8064-7 (e)

Library of Congress Control Number: 2019913592

Print information available on the last page.

iUniverse rev. date: 09/13/2019

Foreword

I am delighted by David Lapin's decision to write this extraordinary memoir. People who first encounter David are most likely struck by his public persona: the deadpan demeanor and humor, the detached tone of his utterances, his avoidance of facile sentiment, his ready delivery of strong, concise opinions on any topic imaginable, and, of course, his understated braininess.

I have known David since 1973. But I don't think I ever had a true handle on the feelings and emotions that, I've always intuited, had to be buried beneath the Lapin façade of remoteness. *The Education of Brainiac* changes all that. In the pages you are about to read, David punctures his aura of mystery to disclose keys to his lifelong aspirations and passions. He does so with courageous insight and considerable wit.

As you will learn, David's life has taken unexpected turns. By the book's end, however, you will perceive a logic tying together the multiple strands. To my mind, this cohesion derives from David's abiding and sometimes unsettling efforts—as of his youth in Puerto Rico and Queens, New York, and onto the years following his retirement from the directorship of the Community Music Center of Boston—to figure out what is best about himself and then to find ways for making others benefit from those strengths.

My own debt to David Lapin is large. As *Brainiac* demonstrates, he has a gift for writing. Throughout my career as a professor, researcher, and author at Yale, MIT, and, now, Columbia, David generously—and mercilessly—has served as my best unofficial editor. He has critiqued virtually every sentence I ever drafted for publication. And when Lapin critiques, you comply! Well . . . most of the time.

Equally impactful is David's broadening of my musical horizons. At Yale in the 1970s, my fascination with Molière's *Don Juan* led me to construct a new course on works that portray the Spanish libertine over the centuries. Naturally, the syllabus had to include Mozart's *Don Giovanni*. The only problem was that despite my boyhood training in classical piano at the Juilliard School, I had zero affinity for opera. With enormous patience during the months prior to my launching the course, David voluntarily initiated me to the wonders of opera and operatic voices as well as to the genius of Mozart's writing for the lyric stage.

Unknown at the time to both David and me, this expansion of my musical taste and ear paved the way for one of my later writing efforts, when I had switched from specializing in literature to teaching and researching film history. That project resulted in *Hollywood Diva,* my biography of Jeanette MacDonald, the legendary soprano of the silver screen—and, not incidentally, someone who David has long championed. Perhaps only Mickey Mantle ranks as high as MacDonald in the eclectic Lapin pantheon of heroes—a surprising duo for anyone except Brainiac!

Unlike David, I am not a baseball fan. But like him, my most dreaded subject back in high school was gym. Yet I owe my current physical fitness in large part to David. In the mid-1970s, while we were both still in New Haven, David introduced me to Yale's Payne Whitney Gymnasium—a huge Valhalla-like castle I never imagined myself, a non-jock, frequenting. Then, three times per week, he instructed me in how best to exercise with free weights and machines. Being David, he of course gave this venture a theoretical spin, informing me that I was "an ectomorph with mesomorphic tendencies"—meaning I was a string bean who had potential for developing muscular definition. As always, Brainiac was right.

But what really stays with me is that—just as he had done in guiding me into what I had thought was the forbidding world of opera—he once again, with patience, persistence, and generosity, passed on to me his knowledge and enthusiasm for a rewarding slice of life I had considered out of bounds. In other words, and as *Brainiac* confirms, he is an *educator* in the most humane sense of that word. *Braniac's* primary story, however, is about David's own education, which he depicts as a lifetime endeavor to attain a sense of purpose that is at once ethical, political, and spiritual.

In *The Second Mountain: The Quest for a Moral Life*, the *New York Times* columnist David Brooks explores how our current culture "inflames the ego and numbs the spirit." He posits that there are two types of successful people. On one hand, there are those who, usually after gaining a college degree, pursue the well-traveled path of career, family, and accumulation of wealth; these folks frequently wind up asking themselves, obsessively, What do people think of me? Where do I rank? On the other hand are those who, often to their own surprise, interrupt the linear existence they, or society at large, had once set for themselves. These are people who come to realize there must be some higher purpose to life than simply satisfying their self-interest. Such realization, Brooks asserts, often comes from honestly confronting one's setbacks and sufferings—past and present, physical and psychic.

The most moving passages of David's memoir attest that he belongs to this second category. To be sure, parts of *Brainiac* can serve as a case study of how to nurture and lead a venerable nonprofit arts institution. (Business-school students and instructors, take note!) But even these more pragmatic parts of the book are filled with portraits of individuals—some mainstream, others quite oddball—who share David's fundamental allegiance to promoting not themselves but the common good.

For a long time, David's closest Boston friends nicknamed him "Grumpy." In recent years we have had to retire that moniker, for David has become remarkably serene. His memoir helps explain the transition. In fact, perhaps the most basic lesson we can take from it, and from David's example, is that ordinary moments of what people generally call happiness are fine; but transcending one's self in pursuit of goodness is even better.

Edward Baron Turk
New York City
May 2019

Prelude

I began this retrospective journey in February 2019 on a leisurely return from Miami to Boston on Amtrak's *Silver Meteor*. I had given no thought whatsoever to composing an autobiography before the moment I actually started to write. And then, it all came out at fever pitch in under forty days. The entire manuscript was written on an iPad without a physical keyboard. I'm old enough to have benefited from a required typewriting course in junior high school. My teacher Mrs. Willoughby's instructive hand must still be at work in my life, though my iPad skills are definitely a hybrid between classical typing and improvisational pecking.

Looking back today, I realize that this memoir has been in the making for over thirty years, when a friend first suggested that I write something that embraced both my own life story and a chronicle of Boston's politics and culture in the nineteen eighties. Those were indeed turbulent times in a city still reeling from court-ordered desegregation of its public schools. My own life in that period mirrored the city's restlessness, as I made critical pivots in both my professional career and personal life. For those readers who lived through this history, I suspect that *The Education of Brainiac* will present a fresh slant on shared experiences. And for those who are too young to be acquainted with this history at first hand, I trust that *Brainiac* will enlighten you about how I came to be who I am. It should also help you understand how the events I describe—both current and long past—shape all our lives.

Throughout *Brainiac*, I aim to be honest, perhaps on occasion brutally so—about myself and others. But to tell my tale truthfully, I need to be frank. The naked truth also yields a richer and more interesting story. Nothing mars a memoir more than feel-good pabulum! As a youngster growing up in New York and Puerto Rico, I would often muse on subjects that I might write about. Usually, I came to the conclusion that my own story was just too ordinary to inspire either fiction or nonfiction. After all, was there anything special about growing up in Queens in the nineteen fifties and sixties? I longed for exotic locales and romantic adventures. Part of this desire was simply a typical teenager's rejection of his parents' world and experiences. Only now have I grasped the everyday richness that I was privileged to experience, not just during those years in New York, but throughout my life. I invite the reader to share in this abundance.

Chapter 1
Girls and Older Boys

Growing up in the nineteen fifties meant one obsessed over polio and communism. The latter I could deal with by checking under my bed for red menaces before going to sleep each night. Polio was more intractable. I had come to the conclusion that you contracted the virus by playing in fallen leaves like the ones that gathered outside our family's home on 206th Street in Bayside in the Borough of Queens, New York. Autumn was a terribly anxious time for a polio worry wart, so it came as a great relief to hear that Dr. Jonas Salk had produced a vaccine for the dread ailment. It was too late for a friend of mine, who was already wheelchair bound. His family lived near Bowne Park, where I was sure he had picked up the illness.

Getting polio from dead leaves was like black people living in projects. Having observed the particulars of my mother's housecleaner, I concluded that's where all black people lived. They certainly didn't live in Bayside, which was inhabited mainly by Catholics, Jews, and the odd white Christian like my neighbor Billy. The Christians seemed to me to possess the most prowess, an attribute that was confirmed in my mind when Billy's grandfather picked up a dead rat by its tail and tossed it into one of the sunken sidewalk trash cans that were among 206th Street's prime real estate selling points.

My best friend was Amy DeCarlo. Amy could be annoying, mostly because she wanted us to play *Peter Pan* over and over. I'm guessing today that I always was Peter and she played Wendy, given the gender conventions of the day. We would fly away and fly away to Never Never Land, accompanied by music from Amy's record player. I had my own record player, but it never really interested me until we moved to Puerto Rico, where I could regularly shock myself on its ungrounded electric current. I can't say that I liked getting shocked, but it did give me the opportunity to test how far I was willing to go to sustain out-of-the-ordinary sensations. Being ordinary was a de facto requirement of growing up in the Eisenhower years, but pushing the envelope didn't seem like a bad idea to me.

Aside from the *Peter Pan* routine, Amy was a good sport and on one occasion, we even played "Doctor, Nurse." She let me put my hand under her red pants and touch her, probably under the pretext of administering the new polio vaccine. I don't know how a six-year old intuits such stratagems, but it certainly felt good, and I liked the feel of her backside. I think I may have rehearsed this exercise on a prior occasion with my cousin Mary Ann, but I'm not really sure of that at all.

A few years later, after master builder Robert Moses had placed the Clearview Expressway through our family's living room, we visited the DeCarlos in Valley Stream on Long Island. Sad to say, the rose was off the bloom by then, and though we reenacted *Peter Pan*, the magic just wasn't there anymore. Twenty five years later, I struck up an innocuous conversation with a waitress at Boston's Union Oyster House. She told me she was from Valley Stream. In a totally desultory manner I mentioned that I once had a friend from Valley Stream named

Amy DeCarlo. She looked at me in amazement and pronounced "Amy DeCarlo is my best friend." I thought for a second about mentioning *Peter Pan*, but like our other mutual pursuit, it just seemed best to drop the conversation and move on.

***

Before Bayside, my parents lived in a garden apartment on Utopia Parkway in Clearview, Queens. We resided on the ground floor under the Lagins. The similarity of our surnames was a source of endless amusement for the Lapins and the Lagins. What I remember most about Helen and Barney Lagin was the stink of Barney's cigar. Also, that they kept kosher, which was new to me. Once the Lagins had the Lapins over for dinner and as the brisket was being served, my younger brother Jonathan ejaculated "Where's the butter?"

Jonathan could always be counted on for high drama. Six days after birth, he had to be returned to the hospital due to hydroceles around his testicles. They had looked large to me, but then, everything about Little Jonny was larger than life. He must have weighed about ten pounds at birth, and he never stopped growing until he reached five-hundred thirty. Even though I'm three years older, I would inherit his clothes, which I dubbed the hand-me-ups. When I visited my best friend Edward Feuerstein in college, I had on a winter coat that had been Jonny's.

I grew to view my younger sibling with a mix of awe and circumspection. Awe because of the weight—"And there goes that Great Leviathan" as the psalmist records. And circumspection because I never knew when he would provoke another family crisis. Here's a sampling of three: after his scrotal inflammation, he developed convulsions, and had to be hospitalized again. (I may have wondered if there was a thirty day return policy.) As a teenager, he would let out uncontrolled screams in public, which my parents stoically ignored. Later on I learned from the source himself that the screams were the product of high doses of amphetamines that the doctors had prescribed for weight loss. Finally, there was the time some years later when the FBI arrived on our doorsteps to interrogate my mother about Little Jonny, who had joined up with the Vietnam War protesting Berrigan brothers. By that point I had left for Yale and was trying my best to tune my parents and brother out of my consciousness.

***

I had two close friends in the garden apartment complex. One was Lynne Neuberger, who I was convinced at four I would marry. There's just one photo of Lynne and me. I am looking too cute in some kind of cowboy outfit with a protective air around me and Lynne. She is adorable in a white linen-like dress that balloons from the high waist to her knees. I loved her. I still do.

Puppy Love

My other friend was Allan Paige, who was twelve. I was kind of his pet, and what strikes me as unusual about our relationship is that I trusted him, an older man. Fortunately I was too young to remember this, but one day Allan lifted me off the ground and dropped me on the side of our house, where my nose caught the edge of an outdoor faucet. With blood flowing everywhere, Allan ran for my alarmed mother and we sped off to see Dr. Megerian, who decided that despite the carnage, the young nose would heal just fine on its own, which it did—though to this day I can see the scar where the nose detached. I grew to mistrust older guys, but in all fairness to Allan, I would have more compelling reasons than a half-severed nose.

With Allan Paige

Chapter 2
Older Women

From Clearview days on, I was surrounded by older women who doted on me nonstop. I think I grew to resent their attentions, or at least devalue their interest. It seemed so easy to obtain, it hardly seemed worth the minimal effort. I have given up counting my aunts and great aunts, there were so many! And they had great names like Birdie, Tante Rosie (who wasn't really my aunt at all, but to whom I may have been closest), Aunty Ann, Sadie, the Bubbe, the list goes on. My maternal grandmother Mamie had fifteen siblings, mostly female, so that accounts for a lot of them. But even on my paternal grandparents' side, there was Aunt Eva, Edith, Becky, and so on. I was trapped in a snare of older women!

Not that I wasn't intrigued by them. They smelled different. They looked big, by and large. And they fascinated me, even as a five year old. Tante Rosie was Mamie's best friend. They had met as silk winders at the turn of the twentieth century in Manhattan, where a police officer once told Nanny (Mamie) not to venture into Chinatown due to the Tong Wars. Tante Rosie had beautiful blue eyes, and she and Mamie hit it off instantly. Both had married badly. Rose's husband Lou Meyer was a wife beater, and Mamie's husband Ardie Steinlen, my grandfather, was a "rummie." Tante Rosie actually introduced Mamie to Ardie. Both husbands were also best friends so the couples saw a lot of each other. Lou and Ardie even went on the vaudeville circuit as a comedy act, Meyer & Steinlen.

Tante Rosie and Grandma Mamie Steinlen, 1956

Grandpa Ardie Steinlen, 1915

Aside from Mamie, Tante Rosie had a good friend named Anna Newhouse, who resembled a better looking Eleanor Roosevelt. I remember Mrs. Newhouse being present when Dr. Megerian gave me a shot up my behind and the look of condescending maternal pity on her face. I stifled the crying, but I resented the fact that she witnessed my exposure. Soon after, Anna Newhouse died of cancer. I wanted to go to the wake—I had never seen a corpse—but my father nixed it. I could never understand why he was so afraid of death. I thought it was neat, but I didn't get to see a real live corpse until my father's father died in 1966.

***

My dad Stanley ran a model aircraft company called Master Modelcraft. Somehow toward the end of the Great Depression, he scrounged the capital to found the company, and it prospered (maybe not the best term) until 1956 when he sold it to the Testor Corporation, maker of the hobby glues that flower children of the sixties sniffed to get high. The story goes that Stanley was done in by plastics. He was an avatar of balsa and his models were made entirely of wood until plastics and their capital intensive production rooted out the last balsa acolytes. Testor came a decade before Dustin Hoffman's encounter with plastics in *The Graduate*, circa 1967.

Nils Testor was larger than life. A Swede who migrated to Rockford, Illinois, he had transferred most of his production to Puerto Rico as part of Operation Bootstrap in 1956. My father's job was to manage the model aircraft and the chemical paint plants, and by 1959, both factories were up and running. In 1956, we visited Puerto Rico for two weeks and stayed in Testor's home with six servants all named Rosa and Juana. Rosa number one allowed me to use the iron, on which I promptly burned myself. That did not make me happy because I deemed myself incompetent in Rosa's eye. Juana—or maybe she was Juanita—had a son who was employed as Testor's gardener. His name, or so I was told, was Flor—Flower, in English. Decades passed before I perceived Flor as a drag name. Flor had lots of male friends who hung around the house, though I doubt they had much to do. Apparently, Testor lived next to a quasi-gay beachfront in a neighborhood outside San Juan called Ocean Park. Testor himself wasn't gay but his mansion did have six or seven exquisite bathrooms.

I remember that because I periodically tried out all of them. Each had bidets, which my mother especially appreciated once she learned that C stood for *caliente*, not cold. One day, Little Jonny ran after me, threatening to sit on me. I locked myself in one of the six bathrooms and got stuck. I imagined my remaining days unfolding in the yellow bathroom; it certainly beat being sat upon for life by the Great Leviathan. While waiting to be rescued by my mother or Rosa number one, I fantasized driving a Thunderbird Junior to Disneyland, which had recently opened. It was the only car I really lusted after my entire life.

The Education of Brainiac

With Juana or Juanita, Flor's mother

***

Baby David had been driven home from Dr. Leff's Maternity Hospital on the Bronx's Grand Concourse in a 1950 wood-paneled Pontiac station wagon. Stanley would soon rid himself of a similar vintage Buick because he claimed it overheated. These were followed by a 1954 Lincoln Capri, a 1958 Volkswagen Beetle, a rare 1959 Borgward Isabella, a 1961 Peugeot 404, a 1963 Cadillac Fleetwood, and others. The one car I haven't mentioned was a green 1953 Chrysler. Stanley and his kid brother Eddie were returning from a trade show in Chicago on an icy Pennsylvania Turnpike in February 1954, just a few weeks after Jonny was born and Eddie had married Aunt Dotty. Eddie, who was only nineteen at the time, may have fallen asleep at the wheel because the Chrysler crashed and Dad was thrown through the front windshield. As a result, Dad lost all his front teeth and became a Polident patron for life. He also lost about a hundred pounds while recovering. Jonny would inherit Dad's propensity toward obesity, while I for much of my youth was the runt of the litter.

David E. Lapin

Ready for an outing in the Pontiac with Daddy

Not that I didn't have my corporal ups and downs. It would have been impossible otherwise given the enormous meals that my mother regularly produced. I remember telling my friend Edward Baron Turk what Sunday brunches were like at the Lapins. He was incredulous, and rightly so! Belly lox, Nova, sturgeon, sable, cream cheese with chives and without, onion rolls, bagels and bialys of all sorts and varieties—all fresh from the baker. Drinks were typically hot chocolates for Jonny and me with or without miniature marshmallows. Then there were the desserts: crumb cake, butter cake, babka, it went on and on with a brief recess before dinner at three. I won't regale you with the dinner menu, but suffice it to say it was equally profligate. In the evening, we would go back to the lox and bagels and whatever leftovers remained. These were not unusual feast days. They happened every week, and while I did my best to keep up with the others, I was losing relative status if not avoirdupois. I was also chronically plagued by gas and cramps. If I was lucky, the indigestion would keep me out of school on Monday, when we would efficiently resume eating Sunday's remains.

Chapter 3
Kitchen Love

My mother Frieda was a superb cook who learned much of this vocation while serving as an au pair to Anna Stabile in the late nineteen-thirties. Mrs. Stabile lived in Jackson Heights, Queens, and worked as a teacher in New Jersey. In those days, married women were not allowed to be employed by New York school systems—hence her trek to Jersey.

Frieda was no more than about eighteen, and it became her task to raise Anna's son Franky and, subsequently, Arthur. Mrs. Stabile's mother-in-law was a first-rate Neapolitan cook, and though she spoke only pidgin English, she imparted recipes by example to her willing novice. To this day, I have never tasted better spaghetti and meatballs than those derived from Mrs. Stabile's mother-in-law. But her real pièce de résistance was *brageole*. A skirt steak or similar cheap cut would be hammered into submission and then rolled with raw garlic cloves and a quarter of a hard boiled egg inside. Tied with string, the rolls would percolate in spaghetti sauce a la Stabile for hours as the meat tenderized, and the room perfumed with smells so intoxicating that it makes me giddy today just thinking about them.

Mom was a very poor child of the Depression. My grandfather Ardie—his given name was Adolph but that ended with Hitler's rise—was never much of a breadwinner. I don't even know if he had an occupation other than hard drinking. His father, Adolph Ludwig Steinlen, was a landowner who was prosperous enough to support three families, all claiming him as father. I only discovered this fact recently through the Internet. Adolph Ludwig may have been a trigamist but he wasn't a liar; he dutifully listed all three families in early twentieth century censuses with himself as head of household. I can only speculate how this discovery has added to my ever burgeoning list of uncles and aunts! My mother adored her paternal grandfather, who lived with them until Ardie and Mamie sued the elder Adolph for a share of his real estate. The litigation occurred around 1931, and when the court threw out my grandfather's case, the Steinlens found themselves with neither a penny nor a means of gainful employment.

My great grandfather went to live with his spinster daughter Lizzie, and Mamie had to find work such as she could. Toward the end of the Depression she moved the family to the Bronx, where she found back breaking work as a super, shoveling coal among other unpleasant and arduous tasks. But that was Utopia compared to the early thirties. The only route to salvation was St. Luke's Lutheran Church in the Woodhaven neighborhood of Queens. St. Luke's not only provided food baskets. Its pastor, Erwin Jaxheimer, became a needed father figure for Frieda and her younger sister Anna. Two Sunday School teachers, sisters Madeline Schoelpple and Christine Hoffman, became my mother's lifelong friends.

Looking back on this experience, I now fully understand my mother's propensity toward feeding us too much. Food became an obsession for her, and she devoted a good part of her adulthood gathering recipes and trying them out first on Franky and Arthur Stabile, and ultimately, on me and my unfortunate brother. In this sense, the Great Leviathan was himself a delayed victim of the Great Depression.

Next to a cornfield with Mom, perhaps in Poughkeepsie, New York

***

My father's family was luckier. His grandfather Harry, the first of us Lapins in America, was a tailor who prospered quickly after emigrating around 1890. He married my great grandmother Jennie and they had two boys and one girl. Their elder son was my grandfather Albert. (I am, therefore, the eldest son of an eldest son of an eldest son of an eldest son.) Al carried on the family clothing interests and founded a couple of dry cleaning stores in the Bronx and Brooklyn. While the Lapins lost money to bank failures in the 1930s, their experience overall was far more fortunate than that of the indigent Steinlens.

My great grandparents Jennie and Harry Lapin
Grandpa Albert is in the middle.

In 1916 Al married a sixteen-year old with the name of his mother, Jennie. Al's parents were scandalized. The newlyweds had not only met at a nickelodeon. Jennie's parents were poor Jews and communists, or so it was rumored. The story is that my great grandparents, the Gabels, hosted Leon Trotsky in Manhattan around 1900. I doubted this legend, but not enough to forego researching its veracity, and in fact Trotsky did visit New York around this time. The communist credentials were certainly valid. When Jennie's older sister Eva died in 1975, she willed a bequest of $500 to the American Communist Party.

Sister Jennie restricted her renegade activity to getting married without parental consent. She had no idea what she had done, however, and her wedding night became a rude and painful awakening to adulthood. Somehow she managed to put off motherhood until my father was born in 1919.

An only child until he turned fifteen, Stanley was spoiled by his doting mother. Like his son-to-be Jonathan, he was also obese. Though he was drafted shortly after Pearl Harbor, he served for just short of a year before being issued an honorable discharge for unspecified medical reasons. When I asked my brother to speculate on the cause of the discharge, he proposed that the U.S. Army probably had had enough of an overweight know-it-all. I have no reason to doubt this reasonable assessment.

Stanley and Grandma Jennie AKA Jane Gabel Lapin

Mom met Dad on a leave. She had earlier gone to work for the Lapins at Master Modelcraft and their Bronx dry cleaners. She didn't like him. Somehow through the years, she overcame her initial appraisal and on New Year's Eve 1949, they were married in a civil ceremony—the only kind possible then for persons of different religions. They spent their wedding night at the Edison Hotel overlooking Times Square, and legend has it that Stanley fell out of bed. If this tale is accurate, it must have made for a mighty splash because on his wedding night, Stanley weighed at least three hundred pounds. Stanley and Frieda certainly loved each other, but the main course of that love would always run through the dining room and kitchen.

Chapter 4
After the Fall

My father's decision to move us to Puerto Rico in 1957 would have a profound impact on my politics, religious beliefs, and sexual identity. With these changes, I also began to intuit that nothing is forever.

Puerto Rico in the fifties was a place where poor people still lived in shacks over polluted streams with corrugated steel or tin roofs barely protecting them from mighty tropical elements. Kids went around without shoes or clothing. And crazy people wandered the streets as if they were in Jerusalem before the destruction of the second temple.

As a white boy from Queens, I was struck first and literally by the wet blanket of humidity that hit my face when I got off Pan Am's DC7 and descended the outdoor stairs from the plane at Luis Muñoz Marín International Airport, a recent addition to the island's nascent infrastructure. This wasn't Queens anymore! As was the case the year prior for our vacation, we stayed at Testor's mansion by the ocean, where I reacquainted myself with the various Rosas, Juanas, and Flor. Something about my mother's body language told me to keep my distance from Flor, but in truth I was much more taken by the women. Each day they would arrive and change into starchy white uniforms, and each day the delicious smell of starchy rice and beans would permeate the house. I was in Paradise!

Living in this Eden encouraged an either/or view of the world. Either you were brown and a servant or white and, well, a privileged snot from the Big Apple. By the time Nixon ran against Kennedy in 1960, my sympathies had been ordained. I was for Nixon. It was okay to support Democrats locally to aid the nice Puerto Ricans (it was only when they moved to NYC that they became mean), but for the USA, you had to go with the GOP, if for no better reason than to be sure the Pope didn't take over everything.

How in the world does a kid develop such views? Easy. I listened to my mother, who to her dying day would deny that she harbored such prejudices. The odd thing is, I still feel at times like a liberal Republican, even though that bird has long since flown the coop.

***

As for religion, well there I really got screwed. Words of wisdom to parents everywhere: do not send your kids to church school to draw Santa on Sunday and to Hebrew school during the week to draw maps of "Isreal," as I spelled it in 1959. There is only so much free choice that an eight year old can process and choosing between Santa and Moses is not among them. For reasons that mystify me to this day, my mother—a devout Lutheran—felt her boys should not be denied the full cultural and religious richness of the Jewish faith. And so, defying centuries of tradition, she had me circumcised by a moyel and raised as a Jew. And I tried very hard to honor that decision.

The Education of Brainiac

Easter 1954 with four-month old Jonny and Mom

My father could not have cared less. In fact, I was by that time in my life growing ever so dimly aware that Stanley couldn't have cared less about anything pertaining to fatherhood. One Chanukah evening in front of my parents and their friends the Schumakers, I donned a yarmulke and began to intone the blessing of the candles. *Baruch atah adonai....* All of a sudden, I heard my father making fun of me to his friends and my mother, snickering behind me and imitating my cadences. I realized then and there that any bond with him was bound to be poisoned. Though I tried to obey the fifth commandment—Honour thy father and mother—Stanley's taunts and transgressive behavior would become ever less fatherly with each passing year.

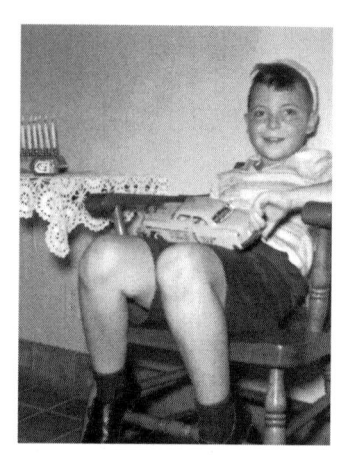

Chanukah in Puerto Rico, 1958

***

Moving to Puerto Rico meant giving up American television and sitting among the elect white kids in Howdy Doody's peanut gallery. But we did get to see movies in English on *Avenida* Ponce de León at palaces like the Metropolitan, the Metro, the Lorraine and the Ambassador. Some of these still dot the *Avenida* today.

The Metropolitan was generally reserved for blockbusters and in 1959, *Ben Hur* played there for a special engagement. I had been primed for the chariot race, and I made sure that I went to the bathroom before it hit the screen. As I sat watching Charlton Heston and Stephen Boyd duke it out, I became enthralled. Something hit me that hadn't been there before. I was attracted to Stephen Boyd not because he was male, but because he was covered in blood as the horses nearly trampled him to death! And then I remembered the stir I felt a few months before when a friend of mine fell off his bike and a small stream of blood gushed from his brown heel.

I took away two lessons from *Ben Hur*. First, I was sure I would get leprosy and that my fingers would soon fall off. Leprosy had become the new polio in my life. But before that happened, I would become a gladiator and draw blood. I didn't rest that year until I finally got my mother to buy me a gladiator outfit for Halloween. To this day, I can't fully describe the high I got when I put on my *Ben Hur* breastplate and brandished his sword.

As an eight year old, my religious worldview was still very much Garden of Eden, After the Fall. I became obsessed with flesh and nakedness, the latter being perhaps my worst nightmare. I would engage in near Talmudic conversations with myself over whether it was more shameful to expose one's butt or dick; I decided it was the former, and let's not concern ourselves with what that means psychologically. Suffice it to say that even when I traveled to Fort Hamilton as a twenty-one year old facing the draft, my main concern was exposing myself in public. Killing Viet Cong, sorry to report, wasn't even part of the equation.

My mother had a prayer book with lithographs of Old and New Testament scenes. My favorite was the Crucifixion, not because of the depiction of Jesus, but of one of the two thieves, whose broken body on the cross displayed excellent musculature. I would take that prayer book with me into the bathroom and do I don't know what. There really was nothing to do at nine years. But I realized in that moment that my life was moving well beyond Howdy Doody and his peanut gallery whities.

Chapter 5
Inertia

Life among the Lapins was schizophrenic in a singular regard. While my brain was constantly overstimulated by cerebral conversations that an ordinary child could barely comprehend, my physical existence at the time is best described as inert. Physical exertion of any kind was frowned upon, and my mother especially took umbrage at President Kennedy's initiation of physical fitness tests for the young.

At the beginning of my tenth grade history class, my honors teacher Mrs. Marjorie Gore asked if anyone knew where the Pilgrim's Chorus came from. I alone raised my hand and responded, "Wagner's *Tannhäuser.*" It was probably then that my high school peers dubbed me Brainiac, a fact I only discovered at my fiftieth high school reunion last year. My mind was a garbage can of factoids, honed from countless hours reading everything from *The Little Red Book of Baseball* to the *Information Please Almanac*. It didn't make up for doing absolutely nothing that smacked of physical exertion.

I couldn't hit a baseball to save my life. I couldn't swim—and this after going to the beach every Sunday in Puerto Rico. I began to feel intellectually smug and superior but physically inadequate and withdrawn. I felt there was a better me inside—the girls still found me cute—but I knew I was playing a losing hand. By high school I couldn't even face the idea of physical education, and I got our family doctor to write excuses for me to skip gym for three years.

Señor Martinez, my gym teacher at the Commonwealth School in Puerto Rico, had tried to get me to swing at a ball effectively. It was pointless. Stanley had not lifted a finger to train me in the avocation that has bonded fathers and sons for generations. The ultimate humiliation was not learning how to swim. My dad would taunt my brother and me by swimming offshore to show how macho he was. His closest call to teaching us was dropping us in the ocean and laughing as we flailed for survival. My girlfriend Ester Fuchs in the nineteen seventies couldn't fathom how I hadn't learned by then how to swim. I was simply too ashamed to tell her why.

David, Jonny and Stanley at the Beach

***

On the other hand, I became expertly versed in topics ranging from Mormonism to Patrice Lumumba. Teachers were forbidden to tell students their IQ, but Mr. Mullally in the seventh grade wrote all the class's IQs on the blackboard—without attribution. Mine was either 136 or 148, depending on how Sandra Yamaguchi had done. I was pleased at this revelation, but I yearned all the more to improve my physical well being.

***

Puerto Rico had been an excellent adventure, but it also proved boring for me and Jonny without the soporific of American TV. And so, after much nagging, Stanley agreed to send Frieda and his two sons back to New York in November 1960. It was probably the worst mistake of my father's life. After several weeks of us fattening at the Edison Hotel, my father's friend Irving Albert found a two-bedroom apartment at the spanking new Park City Estates in Rego Park, or Forest Hills North as the brochures read. We moved in in time for Christmas 1960 and several blizzards thereafter. Rent was $175 per month; the silverfish insects that also found the Estates a desirable venue were an added, free attraction.

Quickly it dawned on my mother that they had made a terrible mistake. She was bereft without her husband, and love letters from that year attest to the loneliness she felt being back alone in New York. Stanley was no happier in Puerto Rico, despite the ministrations of his parents who had moved there with us in 1957. And so, without a job in the offing, Stan joined us in the fall of 1961.

My father had been something of a star in the hobby industry, but on returning to New York, he discovered that there were few if any requests for his services. Various explanations were proffered: he hadn't finished his engineering degree at Pratt

Institute, business partners like Murray Backelman betrayed him, the legendary hobby-retailer Polk Brothers on Fifth Avenue had other obligations, companies that briefly hired him like the Superior Pool [Table] Company were no good. My mother bought the party line. But in truth, he was unhireable because he was insufferable.

Slowly the family fortunes started to sink. Having made good money from our years in PR, not to mention the sale of our Bayside home to make way for the Clearview Expressway, we began a slow descent into the lower middle class.

***

But the descent didn't end there, at least for me. In early January 1962, I developed strep throat. My poor mother of course didn't know that and to save a few bucks, she delayed taking me to the doctor. Around January 15, Frieda's former employer Mrs. Stabile visited us from her new home in Anaheim, California. My mother made a delicious bundt cake for the occasion, which I enjoyed. Around two days later, I took to bed with sore joints and a low grade fever. I wouldn't leave the bed till the following June.

Coming down with rheumatic fever was the apotheosis of my physical stasis. Bed rest was the prescribed cure of the day, as my weight dropped to 78 pounds and my legs atrophied to the point where I would ultimately have to relearn how to walk. I also developed Huntington's Chorea or St. Vitus' Dance. As if that didn't suffice, the enforced bed rest caused a regression to baby talk, and I invented the phrase "Bigi boo, Abbey doo." I have no idea what that meant, but I also devised a kingdom called Oscarland with a parrot as its monarch. The mind definitely does strange things when you're in bed for six months!

The New York City Public Schools sent me a lovely home instruction teacher named Miss Lynch, or Miss Blynch as I called her. She, like the attending physician Dr. Ronald Linder, spent as much time gabbing with my mother as ministering to me, but that was fine. One day, my parents shuttled me off to University Hospital in lower Manhattan to see if anything could be done to speed my stalled recovery. To his credit, my father offered to carry me from the parked car to the hospital. I would have none of it, however, and managed the walk on my own. It was at that moment that I determined I had enough of baby talk. It was time to resume growing up.

Chapter 6
Paternalism

My bout with rheumatic fever had robbed me of interaction with cousins, friends, and anyone my own age. Some parents feared the disease was contagious—it is not—and kept their kids away. I was very close in those days to my cousins Mary Ann and Rosemary, daughters of Frieda's sister Anna and her husband, Uncle Walter. Walter Finck had other reasons for keeping Mary Ann away, particularly if it involved an overnighter. As ridiculous as it seems, he was concerned over the remote possibility of hanky panky. Walter was Anna's first cousin, you see, and I guess he didn't want history repeating itself.

Aunty Ann and Walter were married in 1946 in Stamford, Connecticut, just across the state border with New York, where marriage between first cousins was prohibited. The genetic duplications in offsprings had left Mary Ann unscathed, but Rosemary was born with a terrible cleft palate and harelip. The brave girl suffered through about sixteen operations before Uncle Walter's medical insurance called it quits. The family's share of the financial cost was crushing. Aunty Ann and Uncle Walter both worked for the A&P Supermarkets, she as a cashier and he as a truck driver. Money was scarce in the best of times, so Aunty Ann went on one of the tainted quiz shows of the fifties to raise funds for the operations. Her task was to be saddest sack among all the contestants, whose misfortunes would then be ranked for misery by the live and call-in audience. She had also been given the answer to a quiz question that positioned her for victory. All told, Anna came out on top as the most miserable wretch of the week, and pocketed a few thousand bucks for her effort. Rosemary survived her excruciating childhood, and went on to become a well-loved registered nurse for most of her adult life in Reading, Pennsylvania.

I was closer to my older cousin Mary Ann. She and I would write and direct plays featuring my brother Jonny and Rosemary in the Finck family home basement in Lynbrook on Long Island. I would love going there in the winter to ride sleds next to Peninsula Boulevard, or play Monopoly, or even jacks. Mary Ann was in the avant-garde at least in one respect. She was among the first to possess both Barbie and Ken dolls, and I'm not particularly ashamed to admit that I occasionally liked playing with them. When Mary Ann married in 1971, her fiancé Mike asked me to be best man. I also became godfather to their first born, Christine. Sad to say, Mary Ann and I drifted apart thereafter. Plagued by the family hallmarks of obesity and chronic back problems, she succumbed in 2013. I don't think I was asked to the funeral.

Mary Ann, Rosemary, Jonathan and David in Lynbrook, 1956

***

My other two first cousins were also girls. Renae was born in 1955 to Aunt Dotty and Uncle Eddie, and Lori followed in 1958. Shortly after Renae's birth, Uncle Eddie was drafted into the Army, which promptly shipped him off to Anchorage, Alaska. Eddie was almost more of a cousin than an uncle to me. He was still a teenager when I first recall him trying to teach me how to inflate my bike's tires, and blowing up the inner tube in the process. I was the ringbearer at his wedding to Aunt Dotty in December 1953. Their marriage proved to be a success, despite my father's distaste for his new sister-in-law. And Dotty, like my mother, demonstrated she had more moxie than her in-laws gave her credit for. On her own volition and with baby Renae in hand, she determined to fly to Alaska to be with her husband. Air travel by prop plane in those days was slow, and Dotty must have taken three or four planes before reaching her destination. They stayed through the end of Eddie's term—unlike his brother, he actually completed his service. By the time they came back to New York, we had left for Puerto Rico.

Top hat, white tie and tails for Aunt Dotty and
Uncle Eddie's wedding, December 1953

I never really got to know Lori at all as a child, though I do recall Sunday trips in the sixties to Cadillac Drive in East Meadow, Long Island, for barbecues with hot dogs and orange soda. My friendship with Renae and Lori would be deferred until all of us were well into middle age.

***

In Puerto Rico I befriended a Mormon, a girl whose mother had been in the concentration camps, a boy who repeated himself nonstop, and a somewhat slow girl named "Lina." All of them like me were outsiders for one reason or another, though no one could see that at the time. My best friend, a gifted visual artist who shared my aversion to physical activity, was also the first boy with whom I played "I'll show mine if you show yours." We did it in the dark so I never saw anything.

Lina was to me like Muriel Friedman had been to my mom—today we might say she was developmentally delayed. I kind of resented my mother's penchant for "losers," as I cruelly considered them at the time. And yet I had developed enough empathy from my mother's example to extend the family tradition.

***

There were also two boys with whom I shared physical intimacy. Both were about the same age, somewhat closer to Jonny than me chronologically. "Harvey" lived near us and had an older brother who got in trouble firing off BB guns and getting into various scrapes. I never heard anyone scream louder than Harvey's brother when his father took a knife to his son's arm to remove some lead shot.

One day Harvey invited me into his family garage, where he promptly pulled up his T-shirt and dropped his pants. I didn't know what to do, so I got down on my knees and started hugging him all over. It seemed like the most evil thing I had ever done. Little Jonny would come by and we would shoo him away and resume our sinful ways. For years I lived in dread that this episode would come to light, though the only ones who knew about it weren't telling. I'm told that Harvey became a born-again Christian, so perhaps he's still praying for my salvation.

"Erik" was another species altogether. He was blond, beautiful and tanned superbly under the hot Puerto Rican sun. I didn't know what my feelings toward him were. I did know that they cast me in a new, secret light, and that I was going to be special because of them. I felt paternal toward Erik, and enjoyed putting my arm around his neck while reading to him. Erik's and my parents thought it all innocent, and it was. But I knew something had changed, and that strange admixture of fatherliness and the erotic tugs at me to this day.

Chapter 7
Health Conservation

In 1962 New York City elementary schools ranked their classes by levels of so-called intelligence. So, for example, if you were in 6-1 with Miss Roslyn Jacobson, you knew you were among the gifted elite. If you were in 6-6 with Mr. Harold Moross, well—need I say more. It was brutal, shallow and horribly unfair. Before I left for my bout with rheumatic fever, I had been nurtured under Miss Roslyn Jacobson's tutelage. The prior year (the year we left Puerto Rico), I had been placed mid-year in 5-2 with Miss Harriet Jacobson, Roslyn's younger sister. I suppose the powers that be didn't know what to do with a kid who had spent most of his past in a private school in Puerto Rico, so they hedged their bets and put me in the second smartest class. Harriet rectified that error and anointed me as one of Roslyn's elect.

I prospered under the Jacobsons and after my five month hitch with the home instructor Miss "Blynch," I graduated to Stephen Halsey Junior High, where another ranking method prevailed. Mercifully 7-1 didn't outrank, say, 7-3. But an even more odious tracking system divided the entire school into two categories—Special Progress and Everyone Else. They might as well have called it kosher and *traif*. It was disgusting and of course I was Special Progress—kosher.

Special Progress itself was divided into two categories. You could choose at the beginning of seventh grade to skip the eighth, or you could remain in the eighth to receive enrichment in foreign languages and the like. Maybe because I knew Spanish already or maybe because they were partial to speed (amphetamines for Jonny), my folks placed me in the two-year track. Had I stayed there, I would have graduated high school at the age of sixteen. Halsey's school nurse ultimately would put the kibosh on that absurd ambition.

***

Walking to Halsey was a stretch for a kid who had only recently relearned walking. I had also earned a nasty ingrown toenail from wearing shoes for the first time in six months. In fact, the shoes proved too painful, so I walked to school in sandals that had to be approved by the assistant principal Mr. Harold Pollock. As a compromise with my mom, I agreed to walk alongside thirteen-year old "Carol Brown," one of the school's rare *shiksas*, rather than suffer public humiliation with Frieda's accompaniment. But Carol got bored with me after day three, and I initiated the walk alone, unbeknownst to Mrs. Lapin.

I had been assigned to 7SP3. Most of the kids I knew from sixth grade had been designated for other classes, and I recognized only three students in my home room. Nonetheless, I muddled through this latest misfortune—along with my pus-oozing toe—and got through week one unscathed. We took a test that Friday and on Monday, I learned that my Brainiac powers remained intact. It looked like I was going to score the Comeback Player of the Year Award.

Imagine my shock in the middle of week two when I received a notice to appear before the school nurse. It had taken her eight school days to determine that I was not physically fit to remain at Halsey, and would be transferred to PS 11 in Woodside, Queens, to resume life as a special-needs student. My new class carried with it yet another fine euphemism—Health Conservation.

***

When I applied to Columbia in twelfth grade, I would cite my experience in Health Conservation as pivotal in my young life. I still think so to this day. The class—it was a combined seventh and eighth grade—was taught by a balding, red headed, jolly Irish American named Francis X. Mullally. If this memoir served no other purpose, it would be to recognize this kind-hearted, flawed saint. Mr. Mullally worked with no classroom aides. There was no support of any kind that I could discern. Many of his thirty students had severe cerebral palsy, and seizures would often interrupt regular class activities. And yet he soldiered on as if his calling was nothing out of the ordinary.

My classmates were—special needs aside—a more diverse lot than Halsey's. There were my fellow seventh graders Richard and William. Richard had a heart murmur. Fortunately, my rheumatic fever had only caused a temporary murmur that did no permanent damage. William was the class clown. His best act was twisting his right eye around in its socket, to my disgust and astonishment. William was African American. I cannot recall what his special needs were, if there were any. He may simply have been a "difficult student" who would have been assigned to a special ed environment in the 1990s. On more than one occasion, Mr. Mullally would box William's ear, once so hard that he said he couldn't hear. I think Mr. Mullally was surprised at that. A lot of the boys in Mr. Mullally's class came in for a boxing or two. I of course was not among them. Though I probably could have earned some brownie points with Richard and William, it would have been too shameful. Mr. Mullally must have agreed.

Among the girls were seventh grader Nina and eighth grader Judith. Judith had severe cerebral palsy that gravely affected her movement and speech. She was a remarkable and intelligent young woman who Mr. Mullally chose to recite Rudyard Kipling's poem "If" before the end-of-year general assembly. It was an inspired choice and an inspiring declamation. I could not process finding out two years later that Judy committed suicide. A column in *The Daily News* took note of her remarkable life, and her performance of "If."

Nina was far more quiet. She looked a little like Amy DeCarlo, with dark, short hair and a trace of the Italianate. For whatever reason, I took a shine to her and my first subway ride unaccompanied by a grownup relative was with Nina. There was another girl in the classroom, a pretty eighth grader who I determined was unapproachable. I once summoned up the nerve to nod at her as my school bus passed hers, but that's as far as that romance ever got.

***

Respect for difference is not an easy lesson for a seventh grader to learn. My experience at PS 11 taught me that. It also made me question my smug sense of superiority. There were many changes ahead as I began the mad rush toward puberty, but none proved more lasting for my moral education than the lessons learned in Health Conservation.

Chapter 8

Punks and Thugs

My year at PS 11 behind me, I dutifully reported back to Halsey and eighth grade in September 1963. I was certain a cruel hoax or error had been committed. Not only was I no longer SP; I had been assigned to class 8-2, filled with miscreants and their molls. For a frail twelve-year old just three months out of Health Conservation, it was also the most dangerous place to be. I could understand the school authorities' calculus. They couldn't care less. But why would my parents subject me to such insane folly!

To understand my mother's position, you need to reconcile yourself to the overriding truth that Frieda was descended from generations of good Germans. It just was not in her DNA to question authority. She also must have felt an intellectual disadvantage having dropped out of Richmond Hill High School in the tenth grade. She had no idea how terrorized I felt, since there would be nothing worse in my present jeopardy than getting my docile mother involved.

As for my father, I wouldn't expect his intervention, and none was forthcoming. In that year, Stanley had found employment with the George S. May Company, an "efficiency expert" firm that sent consultants to diverse companies to tell their CEOs how stupid they were. It suited my father's talents superbly, and when he wasn't home enforcing the Lapin Reign of Terror, he was on the road whipping bosses into shape and striking up a romantic liaison with a woman named Kitty.

And so, I was on my own.

The one year I probably should have been excused from gym was the year I suffered through it four times a week. Only the lowest of the low received that distinction. My first week, the gym instructor Mr. Silverstein had us play dodgeball. I had been hit early and was watching from the sidelines. All of a sudden, the ball came tantalizingly close to me so I grabbed it from an opponent and tossed it back to my team. A hoodlum, let's call him "Max," came over to me—he was the one I had stolen the ball from—and pronounced my sentence: "You're Dead." I knew my life was over, but in a Hail Mary, I sought Mr. Silverstein's protection. What a fool I was. He looked at me with snide disgust and did—nothing. His overweight colleague Mr. Koonman was no better. Mr. Koonman couldn't run a potato sack race if his weight depended on it. And yet all he could do when I fell attempting the same was to ape Silverstein and write me off as worthless. It never would have occurred to either to instruct. There must be a place in Teacher Hell for Messrs. Silverstein and Koonman. Sorry to say, my treatment was pretty much the norm those days, and there were those who suffered from their abuse far more than me.

***

Still, I had to do something about Max. Preliminary research revealed he was one of the hoods, which only confirmed my dread. I needed a strategy and fortunately I had one. From years of experience at Stanley's side, I would charm the savage beast into submission. I would flatter, cajole, compliment, assist in his study, persuade when possible—in short employ all the tricks I had used throughout my young life to keep King Stanley at bay. I was Rego Park's Rigoletto, the hunchback jester in Verdi's opera who survives by his tongue, not the sword.

It worked on Max and the thug who stood next to my column in gym. He would regularly punch me—not that Silverstein was watching. Think Riker's Island. One day he looked at me quizzically and asked, "Why do you let me punch you?" I delivered the only reply that would flummox him: "I like it." That was the end of the punches.

And so I spent the next year courting Max. I would engineer any opportunity to get close to him, just to be with him and thus make sure he remained on my side. The truth is that the danger posed by Max and his comrades was arousing. I liked it, and I liked them, as perverse as that may seem. I became Chief Punk to the thugs, and scored my greatest victory when one of them, to my embarrassment, began beating up any kid who dared look at me the wrong way.

I had triumphed and turned Purgatory on its head. Not only would I survive in the snake pit; I actually enjoyed being there. I also needed to come to terms with the growing awareness that my attraction to the Maxes of Queens wasn't a passing fancy.

***

There were of course regular boys and girls. Sometime in October, I was in the Halsey schoolyard and mistakenly began a conversation with a kid I took for someone else. Both were bookish Jewish boys with thick black-rimmed glasses and braces. It was an easy mistake. As Edward Feuerstein started talking, I knew instantly I had made the wrong approach.

Edward had a Southern drawl, having undertaken the northern migration with his father Harold, his mother Sylvia and older brother Kenneth from Savannah earlier in the year. He was different and fascinating because of the drawl, and he was funny, intentionally or not—it was always hard to tell. He also liked old records and as had been the case with Amy DeCarlo years ago, records became our common currency. Before long, Edward invited me to his home to hear his shellac 78s and vinyl 33 and-a-thirds. At the beginning, the puckish Danny Kaye replaced Amy's *Peter Pan* as Edward's star attraction. Come to think of it, there really isn't that much difference between *Peter Pan* and Danny Kaye. Leave it to the experts to speculate on just where that connection leads, though Michael Jackson clearly pranced along a similar path in the 1980s.

Edward Feuerstein, Forest Hills, 1967

Edward and I became best friends, and we remain so to this day. His first semester at Halsey earned Edward the honor roll. I don't think he achieved that distinction thereafter, and it became a great source of frustration to Brainiac that his best friend wasn't regularly on the honor roll. For decades I've dealt with that frustration, feeling Edward isn't sufficiently High Achievement. I became the smug and superior mentor whose protégé just isn't measuring up. This tension between my fondness for Edward and my irritation at his all-too-human limits has fueled our friendship for decades. He also sees it as his mission to cut me down a size or two. In October 2013 we celebrated our fiftieth anniversary of friendship with a gala dinner at Davio's Northern Italian Steakhouse in Boston. Friends and relations came from several states, and we plan on a sixtieth reunion in 2023.

Edward and Brainiac in Portland, Oregon, 1999

Chapter 9

Chaos

There is one common thread that unites most of my closest friends and it is this. Their early lives at home were a living Hell ruled by a totally out-of-control mother or father. Chaos is probably the more apt term.

As you know already, the ogre in Lapin House was Stanley. Possessed with an intelligence that I have seldom encountered elsewhere, he took great delight in reminding just about anyone how superior he was to them. He didn't have to say it. You just intuited it. He rarely kept a friend for long. Like his father who wouldn't speak to his father, Stanley toward the end of his life did not speak to me. And this because I had asked him over the phone to stop a twenty minute rant on fax machines!

The great personal triumph of my father's life was his marriage to Frieda. There is no doubt in my mind that they truly loved each other, and Edward Feuerstein reminds me that they weren't averse to displaying genuine physical affection in front of us. Yet my mother paid a great price for this success. Unlike Edith Bunker, Frieda was no dingbat. But she often had to play one. She also looked the other way at the terrible abuses that her husband wreaked upon her sons. "He's a good breadwinner" was a frequent response to any criticism of her beloved Stanley Lapin.

In 1964 my parents, my brother, and I were lounging in the master bedroom. At some point, Stanley started to tickle Jonny mercilessly, mounting him on the bed like a lion teasing before the kill. Jonny was in agony and I could take it no more. I pounced on my father, pounded at his shoulders and screamed for him to stop. Stanley indeed stopped, looked toward me with rage, and Mom chastised me for not respecting my father. I knew at that moment that, for me and my brother, all was lost.

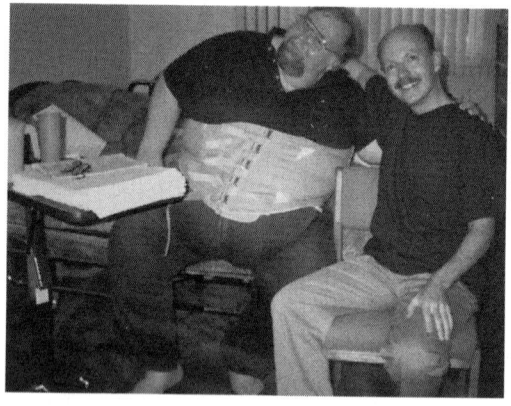

David and Jonathan in Canarsie, Brooklyn, at Jonny's home, 1992

When my father died in 1993, I was in Baltimore at a conference of music educators. I flew to Champaign, Illinois, where my parents had moved about a decade prior. I fully expected to deal with a basket case. Nothing was further from the truth. Mom was already capably handling my father's affairs, and had even sold his last car over the weekend. She didn't cry once while I was there, and I noticed the curious absence of a staccato sigh that she often emitted in my father's presence. Edward Feuerstein is the only one who can effectively mimic her performance.

As part of a husband-wife team I had grown to think of my mom as the melancholic halfwit. Nothing was further from the truth, and yet her deference to my dad forced her to play a demeaning role that she instantly relinquished upon his death. It was a role that came at some cost to her humanity, but it was a role that too many women played within the Greatest Generation.

***

Sylvia Feuerstein emphatically was no Edith Bunker. Born Sylvia Schulman in New York City a few months after Frieda Steinlen (just as I am a couple of months older than Edward), she received a baccalaureate of science in merchandising from NYU in 1943. Years of hard work and night school since 1935 had paid off, and Sylvia became the first in her family to graduate college.

The story unfolds that Edward's father Harold met Sylvia via a wrong phone number. Intending to dial his sister Frances, he rang up President 4-0649 instead of 0648. Somehow he struck up a conversation with his future wife, and convinced her to go out on a blind date to see *Gone with the Wind*. Two years later, Harold proposed at the Waldorf Astoria on Edward's future birthday, January 19, and on May 23, 1942, they were married in a rabbi's home at a small family gathering. (Ironically, Frieda was a domestic briefly at the Waldorf around that time, and she once recalled to me how bandleader Xavier Cougat tried to goose her in the elevator.)

Stationed in the South Pacific as a tech supply Sergeant during the war, Harold had also served time in Savannah, Georgia. Apparently, he liked Southern charm enough to move his wife and two-year old son Kenneth in June 1949 to General Sherman's Christmas 1864 present to President Lincoln. For some reason, the Klan's presence and its anti-Semitic postures proved to be no deterrent. And in fact, Savannah had a modest Jewish community that President Washington approvingly took note of shortly after its founding.

Harold was not a ne'er-do-well like my grandpa Ardie. But his various business ventures as a pickle merchant along with related pursuits proved he was no entrepreneur. Slowly it must have dawned on Sylvia that when it came to wearing the economic pants in the family, she was on her own.

By the time I met Mrs. Feuerstein in 1963, Harold had already suffered a major heart attack. My first encounter with her is now legendary. I was in Edward and Kenneth's bedroom listening to some music. All of a sudden from the foyer, I heard an awful noise: "Whose school bag is this?" I thought I had heard the Wicked Witch of the West. Chaos had descended on the Feuerstein establishment, and I could all but smell Edward's embarrassment.

With Sylvia Feuerstein, circa 1991

Sylvia Feuerstein holds the distinction of being the most feared woman in my life. She reached her nadir in August 1974. Edward had returned from college in upstate New York to live with his parents while pursuing a master's degree at

Queens College. Finishing a shower, he had failed to wipe dry the bathtub tiles. Worse yet, he refused to do so. Sylvia exploded. The caterwauling was so extreme that I—who had the misfortune to be present—recoiled and retreated for my life to Sylvia and Harold's bedroom. As we left the apartment that afternoon, I told Edward in no uncertain terms that he had to get out. And get out he did. Two weeks later he moved from his parents' apartment to West 96th Street in Manhattan and resides in that building to this day.

***

Stanley and Sylvia had their good points. And Frieda and Harold were better than simple enablers. But all four of their sons lived in shared dread of the next parental meltdown. Family composure always coexisted with some nightmare in the making. The same was true with my closest graduate school friends, especially Edward Baron Turk. For Edward, the female incubus was his mother Elsie. A woman who knew no competence (herself a product of abuse at the hands of her miserable father Gene), she imparted no virtues to her three sons except perhaps a love of jazz. Her youngest son Richard committed suicide and her sole thought on hearing the news was that Richard had a gun that could have killed *her*! Her son Edward probably learned nothing from Elsie, who spent most of her days on a sofa with migraines and cramps. Edward's sole culinary skill is boiling frozen peas, a practice he had picked up on his own since Elsie deferred all cooking to her own mother.

I would have doubted Edward's tales about his mother, had I not witnessed her pathology in 1975. Unannounced and unwelcome, Elsie had descended upon Edward in his New Haven apartment at University Towers. Elsie announced she was moving from Brooklyn to Las Vegas after her husband

Sam's death (don't ask why). Instead Edward convinced her to consider nearby Boston, where his friend Philip and a social worker might prove to be of some assistance. This seemed an artful compromise, and Edward and I left Elsie alone while we went out for drinks. On our return, Edward quietly turned the keys to 4B, and we entered the apartment. All of a sudden, Elsie broke into shrieks and howls that rivaled Sylvia's bathroom-tile horror show, though for Elsie—a chronic borderline psychotic, according to Edward's psychiatrist—the screams stemmed from constant anxiety about being assaulted. I could just imagine what growing up with this pathetic and unstable wretch had done to her sons, especially my friend Edward who was plagued throughout his twenties and thirties with OCD and ulcerative colitis.

***

Living with monsters has its virtues. It creates special talents for mediating between the monster and the rest of the world. I learned from Stanley how to ooze my way into people's affections. It also distorted my sensibilities in ways that I still grapple with. Thus is life. You succumb or you learn to deal with it. In general I chose the latter course.

Chapter 10

Last Cry

Edward Feuerstein and I also had fairy godmothers in our lives, who nurtured us into our second decade.

In 1949, Harold and Sylvia welcomed Geneva Ethel Frazier into the Feuerstein fold. An African American domestic, Geneva married Joseph Denmark shortly thereafter, and Geneva Denmark became Miss Sylvia's maid and baby Edward's nanny upon his arrival in 1951. She would stay with the Feuersteins until the family's departure for New York in 1963. Edward has recounted just how hard the separation was on him and his brother Kenneth. Geneva had played the good cop in their lives, and losing her proved wrenching to both boys, especially Edward who Geneva doted on.

My friend C. Thomas Brown, who is twenty-six years younger than Edward, grew up in the New South. Ever the wag, he refers to Edward as "Edward of the Savannah Feuersteins." I guess it's a Southern thing. His Geneva was named Hattie. Edward definitely loves Geneva, who in her mid-nineties still lives in Beaufort, South Carolina. When Geneva finished working on Saturdays for Miss Sylvia, she and Edward would take the bus into downtown Savannah. Even at seven, Edward would sit in the front, while Geneva moved to the back. It was "just what was done," according to Edward.

Geneva had no trouble discerning Kenneth and Edward's difficulty with Sylvia. While it wasn't a question of taking sides, Geneva knew how fraught the relationship was. Not too long ago, Edward and I visited Geneva in Beaufort. I partly dreaded the trip because I knew Geneva would never give up asking Edward—then into his sixth decade of bachelorhood—when he was going to get married. After that torture passed, we settled down to lunch at The Golden Corral, an inexpensive buffet restaurant. Edward excused himself at one point to go to the men's room. I took the opportunity to ask what Edward's relationship with Miss Sylvia had been like growing up. Geneva observed with exquisite tact how Edward had tried and tried all his life to win his mother's love. And with that, her Sybil voice trailed off. Edward had rejoined us at the table.

Geneva, Edward and Me in Savannah, 1987

***

My Geneva was Nanny, that is, my grandmother Mamie Steinlen, who lived with us from the time I was born in 1950. Actually, Stanley lived with Mamie and Frieda, since he had moved in with them at their East 136th Street flat in the South Bronx on marrying my mom. The house still stands, awaiting gentrification from some white boy developer who will want to improve what is today a thriving Dominican neighborhood.

Mamie disdained her Christian name and when my mother was born December 30, 1916, her mother of record had become Mary DeChant Steinlen. (Much as my other grandmother, Jenny, would become Jane.) One played loose with names and birthdates in those days before standardization. Mamie claimed she wasn't certain if she had been born in 1885 or 1886, though the relevant entry in the family's German Bible clearly states 1886. I suspect an early application to Social Security may have been decisive—her monthly checks in the 1950s were $38–and her bronze plaque at Pinelawn Memorial Park on Long Island reads Mary D. Steinlen, 1885-1969. Hence, two fudges have been recorded for posterity.

Nanny was one of sixteen children, twelve of whom survived birth long enough to be baptized. Her parents, William and Emma Kroll DeChant, were descended from German-speaking Alsatians, who had fled Europe during the revolutions of 1848. New York City became virtually a German town by the 1880s, a heritage that was whitewashed during the anti-Hun fervor of World War I. With the family growing larger every nine or ten months, the DeChants moved from Yorkville on the Upper East Side to the Bronx, where William opened a barber shop. William, like his second born Willie, was bald as a bat, and if it is true that one inherits the baldness gene from the mother's DNA, then that attribute is my great grandfather's gift to me.

***

In 1900, following the birth of their sixteenth child Carrie, disaster struck. William contracted spinal meningitis and died.

Without a breadwinner, the DeChants were on their own. Their oldest son George was still in his teens, but would have to make money somehow. Emma, relieved for the first time since 1880 of perpetual pregnancy, could take in laundry and find piecework here and there. Thus it became the fate of my grandmother and her year older sister Birdie to raise Emily, Augusta, Frieda, Florence, Lily, baby Carrie, and the boys Willie, George, and Ernest. It was a tall order for a fourteen year old even with a sister's help!

Grandma Mamie DeChant Steinlen or "Nanny," 1915

Things got worse. Fredie had preceded his father in death from meningitis. Augusta died falling into a tub of boiling hot water. Lily died also of causes unknown. By 1909, my great grandmother Emma was spent. She died at age 59. The miracle is that the others survived at all. While Ernest died in World War I in an explosion at the Brooklyn Navy Yard, the rest lived long lives, especially the girls, some of whom reached well into their nineties. Good German genes, one might say, except for those who crashed (Ernest) and burned (Augusta).

Thus Nanny, via the School of Hard Knocks, was amply prepared for the trials of marriage and motherhood. The former proved every bit as challenging as nurturing her siblings. Still, she raised Anna and my mom Frieda as best she could, and was certainly deserving of a well-earned retirement by 1950, when I was born. Through the fifties and sixties, she would live with us off and on, even moving to Puerto Rico in 1957, when yet another disaster struck.

Frieda, my brother and I were walking along *calle* José Martí to get a bus on Ponce de León for Santurce. Nanny was a slow walker so we left her about a half-block behind. All of a sudden, I heard her screaming "David, David." She was lying in the street losing blood from an attack by a would-be purse thief. He had grabbed her hand bag, she pulled it back, and recoiled into a parked car's steel fender. Neighbors heard the commotion, and swarmed around offering assistance in Spanish and English. An ambulance arrived and Nanny was taken to the hospital where she received eighteen stitches, if my memory is correct.

The incident proved too much for her, and she decided to return to the States and live with her daughter Anna. I was heartbroken. Nanny had always been a treasured presence in my young life, and now we would be separated for the first time ever. Stanley agreed to accompany Nanny on the flight back to New York, where she lived with Anna, Walter and my cousins until 1963.

A strange thing happened then. In a form of parental abuse, Nanny had been allowed to sink at the Fincks into malnutrition and depression. Again, she was taken to a hospital and was released with no particular course of action prescribed. We were at the Fincks's house in Lynbrook awaiting her return. At the side entrance she would have to climb four steps, a considerable challenge in her enervated state. In an astonishing display of indifference, her son-in-law Uncle Walter (who was also Mamie's nephew via her sister Emily), refused to help her, claiming he was too tired from work. It was my father who then came to the rescue, not only helping her up the stairs, but thereafter agreeing to have Nanny return to live with us, where Frieda could supervise her full recovery.

Stanley as you know had his faults. But I cannot recall one moment of rudeness toward his mother-in-law, whom he always treated with the greatest respect. Go figure. Nanny did recover and she lived six more prosperous years until her death from botched exploratory surgery for gallstones and jaundice in 1969. Her demise on March 8 was the last time I can remember having a really good cry.

Chapter 11
Fairyland

Prejudice worms its way to the soul through what the anthropologist Claude Lévi-Strauss called *Pensée Sauvage*, the savage mind. Blind connections and cultural orders are constructed divorced from any empirical checks and balances. And so it was with me as a teenager in the nineteen sixties. Christians were largely stupid. Jews were basically passive. Irishmen were drunks. Blacks were, well, blacks—a category apart. Just about everything and everyone existed in a hieratic moral universe with me of course at the top.

This world had its comical aspects. Heinz Ketchup bestowed superiority over Hunt's Catsup. Even the latter spelling reeked of inferiority. Ditto with Hellman's Real Mayonnaise over Kraft's or, God forbid, Miracle Whip. Just the opposite of what one might expect, Muslin sheets spelled privilege over Percale. Lincolns were superior to Cadillacs—until Dad got the Fleetwood, which demonstrated *its* superiority by being top of the line.

Occasional events would cause me to revise my opinions. For example, when Israel won the Six Day War in 1967, Jews in my view were no longer pushovers. Now they showed strength because in part they got suntanned in the Negev and had lost the pallor that plagued them since their *shtetl* days in the Litvak.

New York City has its own social psychology that promotes these absurd perceptions. A supposed melting pot of gargantuan proportion, it actually encourages neighborhoods to see each other in partial lights that separate rather than unify. Red is separate from orange, black is separate from gray. Woodside is separate from Elmhurst, and Bensonhurst is separate from Bay Ridge. There is no continuous spectrum. The five boroughs may be part of one consolidated city, but a resident of Brooklyn might go her entire life without stepping foot on Staten Island or the Bronx.

I mention this not only to take note of my own youthful moral failings, but also to acknowledge the pathbreaking step my Lutheran mother and Jewish father took in tying the knot in 1949. Intermarriage was a rare bird back then. If at all, it might occur between a Catholic Italian woman and an equally Catholic (if lapsed) Irish male. But even that was unusual. Except for Hollywood celebrities, divorce was unheard of.

In the fifth and sixth grades I had a school chum named Lee Spector who was so smart, he was probably smarter than me. I would go over to Lee's apartment to work on a science project and occasionally stay for a dinner of American chop suey with his mother Juanita. I never met Lee's father, who was always traveling for work. Years passed before I came to the realization that Lee's parents were divorced. There were at least two topics in the early sixties that you never talked about—cancer and divorce. It was as if, in Lévi-Strauss fashion, merely mentioning them aloud would rain their horrors upon you.

***

One small step toward progress in my moral education occurred in my eleventh grade English class under Miss Marilyn Brandee. It was the semester we did Speech or Declamation. I can't remember what the subject of my speech was—everyone was responsible for writing his or her own—but I do recall making a comical aside about the Irish and alcohol. The declamation was a success, but Miss Brandee gently chastised me for my use of the ethnic slur. In principle I could find no fault with her criticism, but it was only when I asked classmate Todd McNamara whether he had taken offense that I felt the sting of my own flippant remark. Yes, he said, he was hurt by my comment. It was the first time I can remember being called on the mat for my own blind ignorance.

"Janos Harsanyi's" family had fled Hungary in 1956. A Park City Estates resident (a further sign of moral distinction over venues like Lefrak City or Sherwood Village), he had been assigned to Mrs. Bertha Mayes' ninth grade English class in 1965 along with Edward Feuerstein and me. We had been placed on the same committee to produce a class report. Edward, a pioneer of multimedia expression (he would go on in adulthood to work in cable television), used his open-reel tape machine to provide musical introductions for each of us. No one at the time thought it any way off limits to introduce Janos to the strands of Brahms' *Hungarian Dance #5*. There was absolutely nothing malicious about it, but the episode does exemplify how our little junior high world was strictly ordered by ethnic difference.

Mrs. Mayes thought the whole skit was brilliant and it was, in its own way. The trouble for Edward was that she concluded it was too smart to have been his creation. I was awarded the English medal that June at graduation ceremonies held at the Elmwood Theater in Elmhurst, Queens. Edward never forgave me for Mrs. Mayes' oversight, but it did give him a lifelong cudgel to hold over my head. Two years ago, I had enough. I fished around in my armoire, retrieved the damn medal, and gave it to Edward in recognition of his contribution toward Janos Harsanyi and David Lapin's triumph in Mrs. Mayes' English class in April 1965.

***

My mother could not bring herself to say prostitute or whore. "Tute" and "hoor" would have to suffice. Ditto for homosexual. Nanny and Mom favored the word "fairy." This would cause the odd incongruence when we visited our local amusement park. To this day, I wince at the thought of my trips to Fairyland, now the site of the gigantic Queens Center shopping mall in Elmhurst.

My father was more direct. Fag was his favorite term, as it was for a pain-in-the-neck classmate in junior high. Jeff called me fag or faggot for at least two years. I had conflicting thoughts on Jeff. On one hand I admired his perspicacity. On the other I conceded that he probably threw the term around indiscriminately at gays and straights alike. I'm not even sure he deployed it as a slur—okay, maybe that's giving credit where credit isn't due.

As an adult I've been asked whether I experienced bigotry as a youth growing up homosexual. Assuming for the moment the accuracy of the inquiry, my usual response has been to say "no." I realize now that "no" is a defense mechanism used to push away pain. How else could one deal with moments like your attempt as a teen to show tolerance for gays when your parent's glib response is "What are you, one of them?"

Throughout the sixties my sexuality would retreat into, if not Fairyland, then Fantasyland. I might dream about living happily ever after with someone, but I never developed any real world chops for translating that fantasy into reality. Role models were nonexistent. Coming out was out of the question, if I even knew then what coming out meant.

Moreover, I was about to experience a catastrophe that put all hope of healthy relationships on indefinite hold.

Chapter 12
Hell

The first time I spurted I was playing Tarzan in the bathtub—without water. All of a sudden, something seeped out. I wasn't sure what had happened, but it looked like the discharge I had read about in *Parade Magazine* that accompanies some cancers. I was sure I had done something horribly wrong, so I went to my mother to inspect the wet dots on my underwear. Of course I wasn't about to tell her how the dots got there, but in short order, she rounded up my father and I was summoned to the kitchen to hear the Facts of Life.

When I was nine or ten, my great aunt Eva—the communist and intellectual—had given me a book called *All About Eggs*. I think the story began with reptiles and culminated with humans. Though Mom was vaguely suspicious of the book, it had proved helpful to a point. I knew that babies formed inside the mother, but I had no clue at all about Daddy's contribution. I thought God decided when couples would have offspring, and that, like Jesus, kids were born through the condescension of the Holy Spirit. This was peculiar logic for a half-Jewish kid, but it seemed to make sense at the time.

Stanley did most of the talking, and for once, he proved to be a *mensch*. He told me about coitus and how pleasurable it was. I was surprised, if not shocked. At the end of the homily, he asked me if I knew all of this already. Not wanting to admit any gaps in Brainiac's armor, I fibbed and told the two of them that indeed I knew much of it. I left the kitchen having covered up for my ignorance but also mightily relieved that I hadn't given myself cancer.

***

I also needed to come to terms with the religious injunction against masturbation. Years later my once Roman Catholic friend Richard Corrieri told me the story of his first coming. Not knowing what to call it, he went straight to his parish priest and confessed that he had committed adultery. "WHAT!" was the priest's astonished reply. When Richard told him what he had done, the father gave him a few Hail Marys to repeat, and told him never to touch himself again. Well, just as with twelve-year old David, THAT was not going to happen. For me and Richard, religion was stopped dead in its tracks, and over twenty years would pass before I could reconcile myself to a less sex-obsessed faith.

Sex was especially prevalent among the malcontents in eighth grade. Bobby Epstein, who sat like me in the back of our home room, would regularly jerk off into his desk to the imprecation "Whip me nude!" His friends would toss around used scumbags, much to the mock disgust of the nearby girls. There wasn't a day that went by when we weren't living out *Portnoy's Complaint*. I have to say it was lots of fun, but it probably encouraged behavior and acts that could easily have been deferred until high school.

***

Nanny's move back to the Lapins had been a welcome change in 1963. But by 1965 it became clear that all of us could use more space. In order to be close to the bathroom, she shared my bedroom with me while Jonny was exiled to a sleeper sofa in the living room. This arrangement worked fine, but it left out of the equation any place in my bedroom to take matters into hand. At fourteen I had exercised quickies in the apartment elevators, the incinerator room, and the seventeen stories of stairwells that hardly anyone ever used. As for the bedroom, I knew that Nanny could hear nothing out of her left ear, so when she turned on her right side at night (away from me), the coast was clear.

But more *Lebensraum* would prove beneficial for all and so the hunt ensued for new quarters. I took the lead and began scouring *The Long Island Press* real estate pages. It wasn't long before I found the perfect listing. 85-25 67th Road was in the old section of Rego Park. Modeled on the tonier Tudor houses that graced nearby Forest Hills Gardens (where the U.S. Tennis Open was played at the time), this was a well-built attached Tudor with parquet floors and chestnut baseboards. It also had three bedrooms!

We moved in around October 1965, and my father immediately got into a fight with the landlord, Max Eisele. Max had agreed to paint all the rooms, which he had done, but according to Stanley, he had also agreed to sand the wood floors. Eisele argued that he had only agreed to clean the floors. A shouting match ensued and for a brief moment, it looked like the Lapins would be out on their backsides, lease or no lease.

Fortunately, both hot heads let off sufficient steam, and things calmed down. But I would hone my diplomatic skills over the next decade keeping Max and Stanley in separate corners.

***

David E. Lapin

Of all the places we had lived, 67th Road proved to be my brother's and my favorite. It had a warmth and dignity bequeathed by a developer who built the home and its siblings during 1931. As a result of the Depression, plans for extending the Tudor style all the way to Woodhaven Boulevard foundered, and the houses that were finally constructed in the 1950s on the remaining lot have no charm at all. I would try to walk past them without looking.

I would say I had returned to Paradise, but in fact a brutal chain of events convinced me I was in living Hell.

One early morning while Jonny still slept and I was barely awake, Stanley came into our bedroom. Before I knew what had happened, he mounted me and began sticking his fingers up my ass. Years later I would recount to my physician Stephen Pearson that his behavior—which would be repeated several times with greater intensity over the next few weeks—was just the tip of the iceberg. My relationship with my father had already descended to the point where I usually communicated at the dining room table through my mom, who would then speak to her husband.

As the assaults mounted in perverseness (I can still feel the disgust when he stuck his tongue in my ear), I decided that I would only let him go so far. He would have to be satisfied with what he had achieved, but I—his son who had just turned sixteen—would also establish limits. Slowly the assaults ended, but for years I couldn't confront what had happened. All I knew was that I felt unremitting rage toward my father—as well as guilt over my feelings toward him and my powerlessness.

Chapter 13
Domestic Tranquility

In pursuit of domestic tranquility, I turned my thoughts to politics and music. Both avocations would prove to be lifelong partners.

Nelson Rockefeller was to politics what Mickey Mantle was to sports—for me at any rate. Rocky was my hero and I devoured an early sixties biography (obviously crafted to enhance his political status) as I would consume Richard Norton Smith's sturdy 2014 opus *On His Own Terms: A Life of Nelson Rockefeller.* Like Mantle, he could do no wrong, or if he did, it was instantly forgivable. Both men could not have come from more different backgrounds. And yet each found a similar key to become stars in their respective firmaments.

In 1962 Rocky was running to be re-elected to his second term as governor of New York. There was little chance of his defeat, but just to make sure that wouldn't happen, my brother and I drew "Rocky for Governor" on two sheets of construction paper, and attached the signs to the cardboard reinforcements found on wire clothes hangers. We then paraded around our Park City Estates apartment corridors in an effort to get out the vote. I'm pretty sure that no one saw us, but at least we had made the attempt. I had become a political activist.

Two years later, it should have been obvious to almost anyone aside from Rocky himself that he was never going to receive the Republican nomination for president. His divorce from his first wife Mary and subsequent marriage to Happy made him a moral pariah to the very same Republican women who found no fault twelve years later with their beloved Ronald Reagan's similar transgression. Hatred of privilege and the sense that the rich play by their own rules—a form of reverse snobbism in my opinion—doomed Rocky from the get go, and with his descent, the once robust liberal wing of the GOP quickly began its disappearing act.

The public humiliation that Rockefeller received at the 1964 convention at the Cow Palace in San Francisco was more than I could stomach. Allotted a few minutes to speak on behalf of some doomed moderate amendments to the party platform, he was booed and heckled for about a quarter of an hour. The intolerance on display was enough for me, and I like many others "went over to the other side." Though I have voted Republican in state and local contests, I have not been able to bring myself to vote for a GOP presidential candidate. When I have come close, I think back to the Cow Palace and the mob that night making a mockery of free speech.

***

Supporting LBJ in 1964 was a no brainer. Barry Goldwater would stab Rockefeller in the back several times after 1964—he voted against his accession to the vice presidency in 1974 and maneuvered Robert Dole into Rockefeller's vice presidential slot in 1976. He seemed to me at the time a rash candidate and though basically decent, seriously unqualified to be president.

I think back on these thirteen-year old's opinions, and have no reason for doubting their rightfulness for the time.

And thus, we got Lyndon Johnson! Has there ever been a greater, more flawed man in the office? If progress ever gives us a time machine, may I suggest that you don't go back to the Johnson years. Who could have imagined the dream that began in triumph with Civil Rights and Medicare, only to degenerate into the nightmare of race riots and Vietnam.

My number in the first draft lottery was unlucky 46. In 1972 that meant reporting to my Selective Service office at Fort Hamilton in Brooklyn. For support I went with a sixth-grade classmate, Richard Davis, who had also drawn a bad number. I had done my homework with the Quakers in Manhattan and discovered in Selective Service regulations that recurring attacks of rheumatic fever or chorea earned you a 4F. It wasn't clear what recurrent meant, but I needn't have worried. My family physician at the time, Dr. George Mihail, dutifully wrote a letter with the wizardly word "recurrent."

As the mental and physical exams came to a close, the officer in charge barked "If any of you have notes from your doctor, now is the time to produce them." There must have been about three dozen of us in the room. To my recollection (which may be off slightly), every white kid produced a note and every black or brown kid looked around with a "Hey, what's going on here" expression on his face.

I had triumphed at gaming the system, but I never felt more shame than when I watched the black and brown boys go out one door, as our white behinds trailed through another.

***

Music had an even stronger pull than politics. Early photos show me playing with a toy saxophone and sitting behind a toy upright, which my mother claimed without irony I called my pino. ("Pino" Noir would become a favorite later on.)

On our move to Puerto Rico, the subject of music lessons was bandied about between Mom and Dad with assistance no doubt from the grandparents. Frieda favored the piano, but Stanley thought piano in the tropics was unwise due mainly to termites. Termites are indeed *un problema Borinqueño* but they surrender before mahogany and ebony, the two most common piano woods. Whether Stan knew this is doubtful, and so my future as a concert pianist yielded to the more practical—and dare I say, cheaper—accordion.

Accordion pre-Beatles was a very popular instrument and I wasn't crushed by the family decision. Enrolled at Casa Wurlitzer in old San Juan, I began on the standard child's size instrument, and quickly progressed to the point where a full size was in order. My teacher recommended a high-gloss Italian model by Frontalini. I got to choose the color. In a burst of derring-do, I chose red over black. I carried that instrument around for three years between home and lessons. The damn thing must have weighed almost as much as me at seven. I've long suspected that my chronic low back pain—a third lifelong partner—had its germ in the judgment that rendered accordion's victory over piano in 1957.

Because of Casa Wurlitzer's relative distance from our home in Hato Rey, I got transferred in 1958 to nearby Casa Margarita, to my knowledge the world's only combination music school-furniture store. This was heavenly because Margarita was not only highly air conditioned; it was also filled with sofas and chaises that I could regularly check out each Wednesday before my lesson with Señor Arias. The Maestro was a kind soul who seemed to need to go to the bathroom a lot during my lessons. I was fine with that because it gave me time to survey his neat collection of metronomes.

My progress was rapid and Señor Arias arranged for me to make my television debut playing *Country Gardens del folklore Inglés*. Right before I started, a title card with my name and piece was to appear on screen. As a crank rolled it into place, the whole structure crashed onto the floor in front of me. I looked at the director, who gave me the PLAY YOU IDIOT signal, and *Country Gardens* came out mellifluously and totally unscathed. I was the hero of the program, and my reward was a hamburger and French fries at nearby Todos Restaurant.

Two years later I had prepared Brahms' *Hungarian Dance #5* for presentation on the same show. But the spur-of-the-moment decision to flee Puerto Rico put an abrupt end to my accordionist stardom. That was fine with me. I already knew I was good, not great. Moreover, a new instrument would soon enter my life.

Almost hidden by my "squeeze box," as Mom labeled it in the photo album

***

Through the years politics and music have afforded me much pleasure. But I needed as a teen to make a compromise with both. Rather than pursue a career in either, I let them become passive entertainments, where I wasn't being placed on the line to be judged. I was a Monday morning quarterback in both sports, an outcome which suited my need to be in control at a time when so much else was spinning out of any. I sometimes wonder if I could have been a successful musician or politician. Pushed to choose, I'm guessing I would have been better at the latter.

Chapter 14
Fall from Grace

Persistent troubles at home contrived to turn me into a cipher in high school. As with rheumatic fever in 1962, 1966 pushed me further toward passivity, ever more comfortable with cynical detachment over self-assertion. I nurtured my role as an intellectual, but avoided all the carefree social and physical activities that my peers recall most fondly about their high school years.

Graduating junior high with the English medal (not to mention the Herbert Nussey Award for overall excellence) had the consequence of qualifying me for exactly one honors class at Forest Hills High School. Such was the logic of tracking in public schools in the sixties. Assigned a track, there's precious little one could do to break out of it. The whole system might crash!

Graduating Halsey Junior High with medals affixed, June 1965

I thought I deserved English and Math honors. The failure to achieve the former made me absolutely incredulous. Had Mrs. Mayes betrayed me? What had been the point of robbing my best friend Edward of the English medal if not to break out into honors English!

I had also done really well in Mrs. Eichler's ninth-grade math class. Maybe—and this is how the system churns away at your stomach and self-confidence—maybe, I wasn't as good as I thought I was. Maybe handling one honors class was the best I could achieve. Maybe my aspirations needed to be brought down a peg or two.

I almost immediately became a pet pupil and star of Mrs. Gore's honors History class—thanks, you may recall, to Wagner's *Tannhäuser*. But in denying me the opportunity to enter honors English and Math, the system was also robbing me of my chances for success on the SATs. In fact, these were the only subjects that counted for anything on those test scores. And so, while others began de facto college prep studies, I was consigned to getting 97s, 98s, 99s and 100s in Mrs. Mercaldo's humdrum geometry class. It was a brain dead year of memorizing and regurgitating imbecilic proofs and yet, it never occurred to her to seek a greater jackpot—the only one that counted.

Fortunately, I found a champion in tenth grade English. Mrs. Rae Kornreich was a gifted teacher, and our first adventure together was reading Charles Dickens' *A Tale of Two Cities*. Tumbrils came rumbling to life. *La Vengeance* knitted her way into my gut. I had tried reading the Dickens novel in sixth grade without much appreciation. But this time I really dug into it. It also didn't hurt that I found Mrs. Kornreich attractive for an older woman.

One day she took me aside and told me she was going to recommend me for honors English in eleventh grade. I was confounded. I must have said something insipid to flatter her, but I questioned whether I was up for the challenge. She would hear none of it, and I moved on to Dr. Morris Stern's honors English class in my junior year.

***

Honors classes, it turned out, weren't necessarily harder than the garden variety. In some ways they were easier. The teacher had a vested interest in your success. After all, it made the teacher look good. It was a rare student like poor Michael, who just couldn't get on Mrs. Gore's good side. Being likable was at least as important as being smart. I liked Michael even if Mrs. Gore didn't. I felt a tad sorry for him, the way Mrs. Gore signaled him out for scorn. I liked his floppy hair, which also must have annoyed the hell out of Mrs. Gore. Mrs. Gore was a terrific teacher, but she did play favorites. Learning that lesson was the key to success in her classroom.

***

Honors classes were for tenth graders. They were also for eleventh and twelfth graders, but by then the crème de la crème had been skimmed off for the latest stratification gimmick—Advanced Placement or AP. Thus proved pyrrhic my ascension to honors English; the real prize once again eluded me. I say real prize facetiously, of course. The lesson I ultimately took from the madcap race to the head of the queue at Forest Hills High School was how ridiculous the whole enterprise had become. Quality of education was clearly playing second fiddle to the obsessive pursuit of getting ahead in a world seen only through a fish's eyes.

By twelfth grade I had mustered enough courage to run for president of the Social Studies Honor Society. My AP status gave me one up on most of the competition, and I won the popular vote. This was a prestigious post as my immediate predecessor had been admitted to Cornell, where he promptly grew an impressive beard. It took me a couple of months to get my bearings but by December 1967, I was inviting representatives from the Nigerian breakaway state of Biafra to speak before us. Other foreign dignitaries from the United Nations followed.

My one misstep was domestic. I thought it would be informative to have someone from the right-wing John Birch Society address us. With no formal nay from our faculty advisor Mr. Drucker, I began my search only to discover that it was hard uncovering Birchites in Queens or anywhere else. I thought then that I had a brilliant idea. I would call B'nai B'rith, the Jewish service organization, for surely they would know how and where to get in touch with their anti-Semitic colleagues. I actually made the phone call and asked if anyone at B'nai B'rith knew how to get in touch with the John Birch Society. A few terse words were communicated before the phone was slammed down in my ear.

***

Without giving it any thought at all, I decided I would apply that year to Columbia University, an Ivy League school with a very small undergraduate college. As peculiar as it must seem given my abusive family situation, I was captive to living at home. I imagined taking the subway each day from Queens to Morningside Heights. Call it Stockholm Syndrome, Rego Park style, I could not make the leap to escape my tormentor. I was trapped in the lion's maw.

I could have applied as Edward Feuerstein did to other local schools. NYU would have been appropriate. Edward also applied to the State University College of New York at Oswego, and spent four happy years there.

I knew before my interview that my chances were not the greatest. My math SAT scores were commensurate with the results for a better than average, non-honors student. Most important, that crippling awareness sapped my confidence, and I could tell from my low energy that morning that I wasn't coming across as Best in Show.

David E. Lapin

Photo application to Columbia, 1967

The young interviewer did what he could to move things along. He asked about my interest in politics, history and music. He wanted to know if I would consider majoring in music. And then I laid the biggest lead egg of my life. I said, "No, because it would be impractical." I could have thrown up instantly. I didn't believe what I had just said; I was simply parroting my parents. I also could tell it was not the answer he wanted to hear. I left knowing I had done myself no good.

It was all over but for the letter. And that—the small letter—arrived on April 15. My Ivy League life was kaput. Well not quite. Eleven years later, as a Ph.D. candidate at Yale, I got to turn down a job offer from—you guessed it—Columbia and went to work instead in upstate New York for another Ivy, Cornell.

Chapter 15
Lost Causes

As Robert Kennedy and Martin Luther King, Jr. were assassinated, as Vietnam was being blanketed by Agent Orange, and as undergraduates my own age were mowed down at Kent State, I was listening to the music of Victor Herbert, Rudolf Friml and Sigmund Romberg—Broadway's leading operetta composers of the early decades of the twentieth century. The conductor Wilhelm Furtwängler and the composer Richard Strauss faced post-war charges for proceeding through Nazidom as if nothing unusual was happening. I could make a better case in defense of Wilhelm and Richard than I could for myself.

While Herbert, Friml and Romberg had been highly popular in their day, by the sixties they were already slipping into obscurity. That was part of their attraction for me. How could Victor Herbert, composer of *Babes in Toyland* and *Naughty Marietta*, founder of ASCAP, and writer of the first orchestral soundtrack for a feature length film, how could he be forgotten! It was an injustice that spoke to my need to champion lost causes, I suppose. And yet, I found an even greater fallen star to save from perdition, the woman who brought Herbert, Friml and Romberg's beloved melodies to movie houses throughout the world.

***

January 14,1965, Hollywood diva Jeanette MacDonald died. I didn't know much about Jeanette, though I knew she had been my mom's favorite movie star. The next day, Frieda asked me to go to Gus's candy store and purchase all the newspapers for their Jeanette coverage. In those days there were morning and evening editions, and some like *The New York Post* only came out in the evening. I aimed for an optimal hour, probably about four o'clock, and purchased *The Daily News, The Journal American, The World Telegram & Sun, The Post, The Daily Mirror, The Herald Tribune*, in short order, several pounds of paper. *The Long Island Press* would be delivered to our doorstep. *The New York Times* had sold out and it was only later that I learned that the songbird's demise had been accorded front page status from the Paper of Record. I was similarly surprised in 1998 when *The Times* crafted a lengthy obituary for her long lived if less illustrious husband, actor Gene Raymond.

From these accounts I learned that Jeanette was truly the first movie musical superstar and the only one to survive the abrupt change in fashion that made movie musicals all but poison by 1931. She was also one of the few musical stars to survive the purges that the censorial Hays Code imposed on the industry in 1934. Dubbed Lingerie Queen of the Talkies in 1929, she made her picture debut in underwear opposite frequent costar Maurice Chevalier, and would go on to greater fame as part of the full throated Jeanette MacDonald-Nelson Eddy team that dominated America's box offices between 1935 and 1942. Her international fan base and revenues for Paramount and MGM were even more robust.

Jeanette's fans had always been unwaveringly loyal, and her memorial service at Forest Lawn Cemetery in Glendale, California was attended by a couple of thousand mourners. *Time Magazine* dubbed it the Funeral of the Year, a bit premature perhaps, given its mid-January occurrence. (Winston Churchill's was also right around the corner.)

What astonished me from *Time's* reporting was the funeral's *dramatis personæ*. Presidents Truman and Eisenhower were honorary pallbearers, along with Chief Justice Earl Warren and Maurice Chevalier. NATO Supreme Military Commander Lauris Norstad was present, as was recently defeated presidential candidate Barry Goldwater. Hollywood royalty of all ranks and ages were in attendance, of course headed by Nelson Eddy himself and topped off by a rare public appearance from the town's ancient queen, Mary Pickford. It was quite the show, and on reading the account, my mother's abiding affection for Jeanette was indelibly transferred to her young, impressionable and distinctly demented son.

The Jeanette MacDonald Story would continue to thread its way into and around Brainiac's life narrative for decades to come. In that regard, I am no different than artist Roy Lichtenstein, critic Andrew Sarris, writer Anita Loos and Playboy Bunny high priest Hugh Hefner. All are on record as devoted to Jeanette. Sadly, none of them has been able to keep the Jeanette torch alive as her music, grace, charm and beauty grow ever more alien to mainstream culture. Still, like I said, I saw myself as a champion of lost causes, America's Saint Jude, and losing in matters musical—as in the world of politics with McGovern, Carter, Mondale, Dukakis, Gore, Kerry and, sigh, Hillary— somehow gave me a backstop for absorbing defeats on non-musical and non-political terrains.

***

One final riff on the music of lost causes. With accordion days behind me, my parents inflicted the next wound on my musical soul—the Hammond organ. I think we bought it at Macy's in Herald Square, and I started taking lessons from Miss Bea Price, a lovely lady with horrible psoriasis and an absolute heart of gold. The problem was, she wasn't a very good teacher. She didn't catch my laziness in playing guitar chords (usually above the staff on pop and jazz music) instead of reading the bass clef notes. This was a bad habit I had developed from my days pushing buttons with my left hand on the accordion, and it seriously compromises my left-hand keyboard chops to this day.

Miss Price continued to send us Christmas cards for the next thirty-five years, but she was expeditiously replaced as my teacher by the more gifted Wally Fields. Fields, I should say, was gifted as a performer; he was mediocre as a teacher, and he habitually smelled of salami breath. It almost knocked me over one Saturday.

Stanley and Wally got along amazingly well, and they would have heated cultural conversations that followed the predictable know-it-all Stanley line.

Stanley:	"Who was the Met's biggest tenor in the fifties?"
Wally:	"I don't know, Jan Peerce?"
Stanley:	"NOOOOOOO."
Wally:	"Richard Tucker?"
Stanley:	"NOOOOOOO. BIGGER."
Wally:	[defeated] "I don't know."
Stanley:	[gloating in victory] "JUSSI BJOERLING!"

Stanley in his Testor days would occasionally encounter Bjoerling, a close friend of his fellow Swede. So far as I can discern, Stanley's job was to keep the great tenor as sober as possible, a truly infeasible project, and to make sure that Jussi would return to New York with the RCA master tapes he had purloined to play on Testor's high-end stereo playback system. Bjoerling tragically died in 1960 at age 49 from a heart attack while vacationing on a small island off the coast of Stockholm. In the late fifties his appearances in New York had dwindled to a few a season, and it's entirely understandable that Wally Fields would be more familiar with the New York based tenors Peerce and Tucker then he would be with Bjoerling. But Stan could claim victory, and that's all that counted.

As for the Hammond, I played it with facility and efficiency. Not infrequently I would surprise myself with extended jazz improvisations that seemed to come out of nowhere. Yes, I played the operetta chestnuts, but I also expanded my repertoire to Leonard Bernstein and Duke Ellington. I even tried my hand at Bach inventions. Years later I would discover the recordings of the great Jimmy Smith, the only musician who could tease from the Hammond its unique musical soul.

Playing the Hammond at 85-25 67th Road in Rego Park, Christmas, 1965

None of it mattered. The Hammond organ, like the accordion, was soon tossed into the dustbin of history, replaced by the electronic keyboards and synthesizers that still rule the roost today. And may I add, unlike the organ, they're a helluva lot easier to move around!

Chapter 16
Betrayed

I finished my career at Forest Hills High School ranked twelfth, I believe, out of a senior class of 1,034 (no joke, the school was on triple session). My GPA was 94.67, and I took perverse pride in the fact that the average wasn't even higher. Brown nosing had limits and, in my view, that threshold began at 94.67. How much more absurdly rarefied did one need to be. I did have scruples, after all.

I also won a four-year New York State Regents Scholarship (thanks to Governor Rockefeller), a four-year Triboro Coach Scholarship (from our local private, pre-bankrupt bus company), and a four-year tuition free ticket to Queens College of the City University of New York. I couldn't have been more sour over my good fortune. Queens was and remains a flagship institution, but it had no snob appeal. I began my freshman year resenting Queens for not being Columbia, despite the fact that I would receive an extraordinary education and incur zero student debt. I actually came out richer by 1972 since the scholarship money that didn't go to books and opera—my latest obsession—went directly into a savings account.

David E. Lapin

In 1966 Aunt Eva had taken me to a post-Thanksgiving concert performance of George Frideric Handel's supposedly comic opera, *Serse (Xerxes)* at Carnegie Hall. Aunt Eva was a Carnegie Hall denizen; in fact she had an office there where she worked alongside her son-in-law Jack Rollins, the legendary agent and producer responsible for the early success of Elaine May, Mike Nichols, Woody Allen and many others. Rollins was married to Stan's cousin Jane, who he resented for having changed her name from Pearl.

I did my homework, and discovered that Handel's famed *Largo* or "Ombra mai fu" was *Serse's* hit tune. I lorded this fact over my aunt, who was impressed anew by my precocity. I sat through the opera, one aria after the last in the Baroque style, without a clue as to what I was hearing or what King Xerxes, sung by a woman, was saying or doing. Basically, it was one huge yawn, if fascinating on its own tedious terms.

Aunt Eva had me spend the night at her West 28th Street apartment with her second husband, Uncle Abe—AKA "the man my mother married" according to Jane/Pearl, who shared Stanley's charm—and the next morning, we went off to Lincoln Center, where the Metropolitan Opera had recently opened its sparkling new house. I was directed by Eva toward the New York Public Library at Lincoln Center, another recent addition, and started aimlessly to browse the aisles.

In those years there were at least as many records as books available, and as I turned away from musicals, I began walking through the row of operas. I thought to myself, what the heck. I might as well try out something. I settled on *La Bohème* with Victoria de los Angeles and Jussi Bjoerling and, second, *Lucia di Lammermoor* with Anna Moffo and Carlo Bergonzi. Checking them out at the front desk, I began the long trek home to 67th Road, taking the 1 train to the D train to the E train to the GG train to the Q11 bus, basically the torturous route I would have traveled daily if Fortune had favored me with Columbia.

I got home and listened to *La Bohème*. Wow. I don't know if it was my parents' Miracord turntable and Bogen amplifier or the dulcet voices of de los Angeles and Bjoerling or the heartbreaking story about the silk flower embroiderer Mimì and the poet Rodolfo. It didn't matter. Whatever it was, my life had changed. Having repressed so much emotion from junior high forward, I was now transported to another realm where erotic urgings are sublimated into full throated song. There was no going back. I became and remain a dyed-in-the-wool opera fanatic.

***

In retrospect I see my mother's love affair with Jeanette MacDonald as having paved the way for my newest passion. Listening to Jeanette's records had afforded me the opportunity to experience the heightened expressiveness of the trained human voice, sopranos particularly. It was, therefore, not a big leap for me to dive head first into the world of opera. It was also not an especially rare thing for Jewish and Italian kids in the New York City of the 1960s and 70s to love opera. If it wasn't in their genes, it was on their radios, record players and televisions—a distinctly different reality than what prevails today.

Still, the Metropolitan was a daunting place for any teenager. I wouldn't summon up the nerve to enter its hallowed auditorium until Halloween 1970 when, at age nineteen, I bought tickets for my friend Georgette Gestely and her parents for a gala performance of *La traviata* with superstars Joan Sutherland as Violetta, Carlo Bergonzi and Robert Merrill. It was a special night in Met history. The well-loved baritone Merrill was celebrating his twenty-fifth anniversary with the company and eight of his sixteen past Violettas trooped on stage to salute him. It was an opera neophyte's dream and Georgette, her parents and I—along with four thousand fans—got to see Licia Albanese, Anna Moffo, Renata Scotto and Renata Tebaldi in one fell operatic swoop.

As if that wasn't sufficient, Mayor John V. Lindsay entered the parterre boxes with Israel's prime minister Golda Meir on his arm. The house went wild and I, way up in the *altissimo* balcony boxes, could not have imagined a more thrilling high.

***

Back at Queens I spent my first two years taking everything from astronomy (about which I can recall absolutely nothing) to contemporary civilization (What makes a classic classical?) to modern literature from James Joyce to F. Scott Fitzgerald to William Faulkner. I was excited by Joyce, bored by Fitzgerald (still am) and completely defeated by Faulkner, whose *Sound and the Fury* I must reread someday.

I also began to take some powerful courses in economics. I had arranged to take *Introduction to Macroeconomics* with Professor Tsimbinos on Saturdays from nine to noon. This gave me enough time to get home, have lunch and prepare for Milton Cross and the *Texaco-Metropolitan Opera*, a staple of national broadcasting since 1940. (The broadcasts, themselves, with different sponsors reach back to 1931.)

I got an A of course and immediately registered for *Microeconomics* with a brilliant instructor named Robert Lissack, who had spent time consulting with oil companies in the Persian Gulf. Lissack got me hooked on applied differential calculus, Pareto optimality, indifference curves, and, yes, the Point of Constrained Bliss, a phrase that only an economist could adore. With Robert Lissack I found myself as much in Seventh Heaven as I had been with Joan Sutherland at the Met.

The most attractive element of microeconomics for me was its condescension toward reality. As in so many of Brainiac's endeavors, it allowed me to fly unhinged—and I loved it. With yet another A in my pocket, I went immediately to the department's professor of price theory, which I determined would be my life métier. The class was already oversubscribed and he respectfully declined my entreaty. I could not change his mind, since he reasoned correctly that I could take it the following semester.

In an *Augenblick*, I felt betrayed, jilted, and crushed. My love affair with economics was over and, on the quickest of rebounds, I fell into political science's welcoming arms. Besides, it was easier.

Chapter 17
Summers of Discontent

Summers could be occasions for elation and despair. Despair if there was nothing like a job to occupy my time. Elation once something came into focus to structure July and August.

As a child in Puerto Rico, we would be whisked away once school was over and moved to Manhattan, where Frieda would set up shop with her two boys in a hotel for eight weeks. I can only imagine the cost of these escapades. One summer we stayed in the Bronx at Uncle Eddie and Aunt Dotty's apartment while they were in the Catskills. That mustn't have worked out too well because the next year we were plopped back in Manhattan at the Hotel Olcott on West 72nd Street.

Our first summer in New York found the Lapins (*sans* Stanley except for the last week or two) at the Hotel Bryant on Broadway around the corner from the Ed Sullivan Theater, then known as Studio 50. The Bryant, now the Ameritania, was home to actors, retirees, and eccentrics. We fit in just fine. Our suite was large and Jonny and I loved going up and down in the several elevators, which were still manned by professional operators in uniform.

Among the permanent residents was a family of jugglers who had appeared on *The Ed Sullivan Show*. Apparently, their glory days were behind them, since the father spent most afternoons in front of the television watching Yankees games. (The Dodgers and Giants had already fled to the West.) His daughter Christine became my pal, and my first excursion to Central Park to check out the Zoo and its nearby granite rocks was with Jonny and her. We had a great two months together, drinking Kool Aid and eating Arnolds Bakery's lemon cookies. There was also a drink called Fizzies, which you dunked in water like Alka Seltzer. The world was a happy place as I made acquaintance with penny arcades, Horn & Hardart Automats, and the ever present smell of urine in the city's IRT, BMT and Independent or IND subway stations. Once, Uncle Walter took Jonny and me to Planter's Peanuts in Times Square where we licked our way through mounds of peanuts on top of vanilla ice cream cones. I remember passing the musical *West Side Story* at the Winter Garden on our way for the ice cream. Later, when my father joined us at the beginning of August, he rented a two-door yellow Cadillac Convertible. We drove around the Big Apple in that dream coupé for almost two weeks. For a seven year old, summers couldn't get any better.

***

And they didn't. The next two years were kind of anticlimactic after our first northern excursion. The Bronx had Yankee Stadium and the Bronx Zoo, but getting from the mainland borough into Manhattan proved to be a daily drag. Also, there was no Cadillac redux that year. The final summer in Manhattan was better, but the most vivid memory I have of that season was spilling not one but two Coca Colas at the same lunch in a diner near the Olcott. I'm sure I empathized with my poor mother as Coke number two went flying across the table. She would have done anything to have been under it by then.

On our return to living full time in New York, summer vacations abruptly ceased to exist. Park City Estates had a swimming pool, but we didn't even avail ourselves of that option. We did nothing but eat and sleep. We didn't go anywhere (except to local attractions like the Rufus King Manor in Jamaica, Queens) and I didn't make any special summer friends like Christine. For years I surmised that this abrupt change had something to do with our family's sagging finances. But that only tells a partial tale. The more compelling cause was my father's faint desire to do anything as a family. In fact, it was his extended absence that had made our New York holidays possible. Not surprisingly, once Jonny and I had flown the coop, Stanley and Frieda resumed their summer vacations.

Meanwhile, several years of doing nothing took its toll, and my first bouts of mild depression came as I would confront the annual reality of yet another empty summer. Just what a teenager wants to do; geez, we didn't even go to Jones Beach!

Salvation finally came through employment, and in 1967 I started my first job—dachshund walking aside—as a runner on Wall Street. There were fulltime messengers for all the banks and brokerage houses back then, and their ranks were supplemented each July and August by high school kids with fresher legs. I guess this gave the older guys time to take their own vacations, but I distinctly recall being mentored by some who hung around to show us the ropes.

It was a heady business hauling around millions in securities and going to brokerage houses, most of which no longer exist. Mine was named Halle & Stieglitz, a boutique firm presided over by the venerable Stanley Halle, who came to work each day in a Hamburg. I've never had a thing for older men, but add wealth to the picture (as with Testor) and I was slobbering all over him with courtesies and compliments. I didn't expect anything in return, and that's just what I got. I did make enough money to buy my first complete opera recordings—once again, starting with *Lucia di Lammermoor* though this time with Roberta Peters and Jan Peerce. And I did discover one could eat lunch for a dollar at Chock full o'Nuts. Pretty good hot dogs, too, though they were purchased more for their lack of cost than their taste. I had definitely inherited Grandpa Al's penny pinching ways.

***

Still, as each school year came to a close, I would be desperate to find something—anything—to do over the summer months. And in 1970 I hit the jackpot. That spring I had completed an internship with the New York City Department of Rent & Housing Maintenance, thanks to my Queens College political science mentor Madeleine Wing Adler. Madi was an acquaintance through her then-husband Norm of the Department's commissioner Benjamin Altman, and she inveigled the internship from him. I'm not sure how or why that positioned me for a paid summer gig, but I asked the Honorable Altman for a remunerative position and he gave it to me.

And quite the job it was. I would serve summonses for housing code violations throughout Brooklyn. Each morning I reported downtown to Court Street, and from there I would branch out to the far reaches of the borough, teamed with another beneficiary of the City's summer largesse, "James Blake." Blake was an undergraduate at Manhattan College, a good Catholic boy as our elders said at the time. Fortunately, James knew more about Brooklyn than I did, and we steered away from confronting some particularly shady figures and neighborhoods.

Most of the time we'd give warrants to unsuspecting superintendents or tenants whose landlords had placed their names instead of their own on the city's housing registration lists. That was a bummer, but if their name was on the official list, they were served regardless. Many of the violations were utterly innocuous, like having a lightbulb with insufficient wattage at the building entrance. The problem with the system was that it called for the same response whether the violation was a broken lightbulb or a broken boiler. Whatever the violation, the named defendant had to appear in housing court to respond. Correcting the violation might get the violation voided, but it didn't automatically excuse you from a court appearance.

We tried mightily to be as flexible as possible, but under the circumstances, it was no wonder that some folks got overheated, like the otherwise nice black lady who ran after me one afternoon with a butcher's meat cleaver. It was all in a day's work—except once.

We were in the largely Italian neighborhood of Red Hook and were about to walk past a well manicured lawn toward a modest house conspicuously set apart from its neighbors. I was prepared to do my duty when James pulled back. "Uh, let's pass on this one," he muttered cryptically. "Okay," I responded as we walked away. Only later did he reveal that our target was Mary Gallo, mother of Joey Gallo of the Profaci-Colombo crime family. Joey was mowed down at Columbus Circle the following June. As for James and me, we decided to bury the Gallo summons deep in the borough's coldest case files, where it may well reside to this day.

***

That summer I was asked out by another one of my young co-workers, also named David, to attend a performance of the Mostly Mozart Festival at Lincoln Center, then in its fourth season. There was nothing untoward about his invitation. We'd be going as a group with some of his friends. And yet, I was so afraid of his coming on to me—or that his friends were gay—that I turned down his offer. Complaining about how little I had to do in the summer, I foreclosed on a nice time out with some guys or perhaps even the possibility of making a new friend. Such was the state of Brainiac's rudimentary social skills as I teetered on a new chapter that forebode similar challenges directly ahead.

Chapter 18
Political Romance

Though I never got a grade below an A in economics, it did require some effort. The same could not be said for most political science courses—with one exception, *The American Presidency* with Professor Sol Resnik. Sol was a Korean War veteran, an experience that did nothing to deflect him from old left political leanings. He saw capitalism's quicksand beneath every political institution, the presidency especially, and a course with Sol Resnik was nothing if not a detective story in following the money.

He was also a ball breaker. A few years ago, I got an email out of the blue from Kenny Feder, another Resnik student. He wanted to confirm forty years after the fact that I actually got an A in *The American Presidency*; that's how rare Resnik's A grade was. I replied in the affirmative, but only by shirking my efforts in just about every other course that semester, especially Willy Withers's class on *Public Finance.*

Somewhere I still have my term paper for Sol on the presidency. It focuses in magnificent if mind-numbing detail on how presidential power arises historically from the budgetary process and the growth of agencies that ostensibly regulate corporations and interstate commerce. Sol was not much of a political scientist. His approach was essentially historical, and my paper was crafted to cater to his tastes. I almost plotzed when it came back with an A- grade. I had climbed Mount Resnik and was poised to plant the Lapin flag on its peak. Which is precisely what happened when I got a final A for the term. I had reached the Point of Constrained Bliss, political science style.

Resnik had surgery for lung cancer in 1972. He asked me to become his aide, and I spent that summer getting him between his apartment on West 101st Street and Riverside Park, where he wanted to enjoy the afternoons. I never got used to the smell of dog pee, which was omnipresent back then. I guess the cancer or the chemo had canceled Sol's olfactory sense. We talked about many things. The conversation I recall most vividly was about the operas of the twentieth century Czech composer Leoš Janáček. I gave him my recording of *Katya Kabanová* as a going away present that August. No longer climbing Mount Resnik, I just wanted him to love the drama and the music.

***

Madi Adler was a recent addition to the faculty with a doctorate in hand from the University of Wisconsin. Unlike Sol, she was comfortable with mainstream political science and its empirical main currents. My first data analysis for Madi was done with IBM punch hole cards, though I have no memory of the subject—probably some voter survey analysis of no consequence. If it could be measured, it wasn't worth knowing, thought snarky young Lapin. I realize now that this view, legitimate or otherwise, would not do much to endear me to my future political science colleagues. But that's a tale for another chapter.

Madi could not have been more solicitous of her students, and she quickly developed a fan base that rivaled Sol's merry masochists. She and Norm would have us over to their Bronx apartment. In the summers, we visited them in rural northwest Connecticut, where I rode a horse for the first time and developed blinding hay fever. I was such a city critter and still am.

It was also due to Madi that I got into the University of Chicago, MIT, and Yale for graduate school. In truth, I had no strong feelings about extending my political science career. I liked the intellectual badinage, but that was about it. Ditto for law school. I dutifully applied to Georgetown, NYU and the University of Pennsylvania, got into the first two and was waitlisted at Penn when I withdrew my application to accept Yale's offer. MIT had been in hottest pursuit, and even got two of their biggest guns, Walter Dean Burnham and George Rathjens, to woo me. Nothing doing, thought I. Yale would make up for the Columbia fiasco, and I decided for that reason alone to head to New Haven and my first sleepaway school in September 1972.

***

Madi was also responsible for introducing me to Ester Fuchs, a student one year younger than me who would play a lead role in my life for almost a decade. Even now a day hardly passes when I don't think about her.

A resident of the Bayside neighborhood where we lived before the move to Puerto Rico, Ester was part of an orthodox Jewish family with ties to the synagogue where my mother went to register me in 1955. She was outraged when I told her the story of the rabbi informing Frieda that she should consider enrolling me in church instead. I liked Ester's claims on the world's injustices and we quickly began seeing each other on a regular basis outside the classroom.

Unlike Georgette Gestely (who I considered strictly a friend), I had romantic feelings toward Ester. She was smart, very striking with dark hair in the Amy DeCarlo tradition, and surprisingly with-it, given her family's strict religious traditions. The Fuchses were the kind of family that unscrewed the refrigerator light bulb before *Shabbos*. When we went out on a date, Ester would often carry a tuna fish can in case we couldn't find a kosher restaurant. Life with Ester was intriguing, exhilarating and exasperating, and it was just that combination that attracted me to her.

In our senior year, the two of us headed for spring break to Miami Beach. We stayed at a fleabag hotel called the Churchill or Churchill Arms or some such thing. It was in the section of the city where religious Jews stayed. My first day on the beach was nearly my last. I got so sunburned that my feet turned purple. I was incredibly embarrassed, but Ester took it in stride. I still treasure a silver teaspoon that I filched from some prior resident's stay at the Churchill.

I actually could never figure out what Ester saw in me. She could have had her pick of any number of suitors. Why would she fixate on a *shaygetz*, a non-Jewish boy? Okay, strictly speaking, I was a half-Jew, but even her Bayside rabbi had difficulty with that. What is more, our intense conversations must have betrayed growing ambivalence about my faith. Then again, why was I attracted to her? Though I had never acted on them, I clearly was a *goy* with gay inclinations. It didn't matter, at least as far as I was concerned.

Graduate school separated us, and by 1980, it was time to put an end to any pretense that we were still a couple. To this day,

I regret the letter I sent ending our relationship. Some part of me still wishes that it could have been otherwise. Ester went on to become a prominent professor of political science at, you guessed it, Columbia University. She married and recently one of her sons tied the knot with the man of his dreams.

Ester at 85-25 67th Road

Chapter 19
Yale

I graduated Queens College *magna cum laude* with a 3.797 GPA, or three one-thousandths of a point from *summa*. Madi offered to change my last grade with her from A to A+ to put me over the top, but as was the case at Forest Hills High School, I refused to game the system, or at least tweak it any more than I had already. In deference to my mother's entreaties, I did join *Phi Beta Kappa* and its gold key remains in my possession to this day. I also left as president of *Pi Sigma Alpha*, the Political Science Honor Society.

None of this prepared me for Yale. Once again, as with Little Jonny, I felt like I was the runt of the litter. Not only were my fellow classmates older than me, most had spent a year or two polishing their CVs with internships and jobs in government. Only Steve Bachman, a graduate of Boston Latin School and Harvard, was my age. I quickly surmised that I must have been at the bottom of the 1972 recruitment barrel. Nonetheless, I had made it in and nothing was going to tarnish my victory.

That summer I had bought a new wardrobe at Bloomingdale's, including a silk shirt with *Art Nouveau* ladies plastered all over it from the collar to the tails. I must have looked perfectly ridiculous, what with the shirt, bell bottom corduroys, a Prince Valiant hairdo and a Fu Manchu mustache. In my defense, everyone looked at least slightly spooky in 1972, so I wasn't alone in that regard.

The first reception for incoming students was held at Brewster Hall on Prospect Street, then the home of the Department. Cheese and crackers were served along with Thunderbird wine; apparently no expense was spared. Joseph LaPalombara, the chairman, welcomed everyone with the news that he'd be delighted if we were gone in three years, but watch out if we hung around for five. Everyone chortled, though half the class was destined to fall into the five plus dumpster—including me.

I made friends at the reception with Morris McCain, who had studied Comparative Politics at Oxford and Soviet Politics at Princeton. There was nothing straight or gay about McCain's appearance, and I hadn't a clue when we struck up our first conversation that he way gay. At any rate, I would move in with him and his boyfriend the following summer, and Morris became the first person I came out to.

With Graduate School colleagues Morris McCain, left, and Lode Willems

***

My first misstep was not taking the Political Science data analysis course, opting instead for an offering in the Statistics Department. This pick pegged me as someone who didn't play by conventional rules, which was true. I had a hard time with the notion that empirical data had much to offer political science. Unlike economics, political data seemed wishy washy, voter surveys and roll call analyses being prime culprits. Nonetheless, it was political SCIENCE, and unless I was going to pursue the arcane road of political PHILOSOPHY (shudder), I would have to make my peace with the empiricists, something I never really achieved.

I liked statistics, and I lucked out in gaining a tutorial with the Statistics Department chairman, Francis Anscombe, a dotty Englishman who had me analyzing rain levels in Storrs, Connecticut. I loved it—it was the only course that first semester I totally enjoyed. I wound up with an Honors grade, my only such distinction in my first term, though not from my own department.

The three poli sci courses had their charms. Stanley Greenberg, who would go on to become one of the nation's leading Democratic pollsters, gave a course called *Political Mobilization in Poor Neighborhoods*. It was alright though nothing special—precisely the kind of course you'd expect from a young assistant professor whose first graduate course was modeled on his own dissertation.

James Fesler was at the opposite end of the career spectrum from Greenberg. A long time scholar of public administration, one of the least esteemed subdisciplines in political science (probably because it has to do with something real), Fesler was already a dinosaur when I took his class. We were a seminar of about eight or nine. Led by the august professor smoking a cigar, and followed by half the class smoking either cigars or pipes, the room would often seem to float. It was hard keeping my balance in the haze, though I did manage to impress Fesler once with a paper on redundancy in bureaucratic organizations. I didn't feel it was necessary to add redundancy to administrative systems since their inherent tendency toward duplication and waste should suffice. Cool?

Finally, there was the charlatan David Apter, who had me read Georg Lukacs and Antonio Gramsci my first month at Yale. If anyone understood a sentence out of Apter's mouth, there must have been something wrong with you. Apter had done his early work as a political ethnographer, turning out legitimate studies on the then-new nation state of Uganda and the politics of modernization. Somewhere along the way, he fashioned himself a theorist of political development, and began drinking the French Kool Aid of structuralism and critical theory. By the time I encountered him, Apter had penned a curious tome called *Choice and the Politics of Allocation*. The book was as indecipherable as the title. It had something to do with consummatory versus instrumental values, the latter being dominant in western democracies. There were a few words of wisdom that one could cull from reading *Choice and the Politics of Allocation*, but basically everyone including Apter, I surmise, knew it was a sham. That's what I hated about political science. The very professors who droned on about their minions' needs to do empirical data analysis would flee that servitude as fast as they could for empirical theory, whatever that was supposed to mean.

Two David Apter stories for the record. When I was searching for a dissertation advisor for an aborted thesis on campaign finance, I made a courtesy call on Apter on the off chance that he might prove insightful, if not actually helpful. By the end of our hour together, he had decided that I need to jettison my stated interest and go to Sweden to study consummatory and instrumental values in the Welfare State. No thanks.

Then there was the comic *tête-à-tête* between Apter and the Olympian Sterling Professor Robert Dahl. Dahl's middle name should have been Condescension. In one of those accidents that happens in academic hallways, Apter and Dahl unintentionally bumped into each other. I was witness to this collision of the giants. I suspect they had been avoiding each other for eons. Anyway, *politesse* prevailed and Gentleman Bob said to Apter: "We must get together for coffee sometime," to which Apter replied, "Yes, of course," and proceeded on his merry way.

Yeah, right. Now in which century do you that *kaffeeklatsch* took place?

Chapter 20
A Hothouse

Spring semester 1973 witnessed a return to my winning ways—three Honors grades and one High Pass—but by then my antennae were turning back toward music. I lucked out in that Leonard Bernstein had sanctioned two performances of *Mass*, his latest *succès de scandale,* at the Yale School of Drama. President Nixon had declined to attend the 1971 world premiere at the Kennedy Center for fear that the staging would contain anti-Vietnam War screeds. He needn't have worried. *Mass* is a highfalutin cousin to the musical *Hair*, a riff on the Tridentine Mass with both embarrassing and moving pop-rock interpolations. Wags at the Drama School dubbed it *Mess*.

Once again, I assumed my armchair position of disinterested observer. The only thing I put on the line—usually over pizza at Naples or Yorkside Restaurants—was disdain for the entire enterprise. Still, I was fascinated how the production came together with Yale grit and savvy. If the music was dreck (much of it isn't), the young singers and musicians were all terrific. The results were performances that probably exceeded the Kennedy Center premiere, and the cast was invited by Bernstein that summer to give the show its European premiere in Vienna. As for me, I was impressed in spite of myself.

The only connection I had to the show was one of its featured players, Annette Insdorf. Annette and I had gone to junior high, high school and college together and yet we never became close until we met again at Yale. By the end of our first year, we were friends for life and more.

Annette is the most efficient writer I know. Her dissertation on writers from Ralph Waldo Emerson to John Dewey was essentially hatched while she was still an undergraduate at Queens. Schmoozing her way into the good graces of English Department guru Harold Bloom, she dispatched the thesis in time to earn her doctorate in three years with the Venerable Bloom as advisor. By then, she had already begun her own transcendental move from literature to film, with a focus on French New Wave directors, François Truffaut especially. She became an authority on Truffaut and subsequently wrote a leading English language book on his life and works.

Somehow—and this is for Annette's memoir, not mine—she also cobbled together a full-time appointment teaching film in the departments of English, French, American Studies, and East European Studies! I cannot emphasize just how rare this appointment was in Yale history. To hire one's own is not the norm; to hire one's own in a different discipline—well, you get the point. And yet, for Annette, it was just another stepping stone that culminated in tenure at my old bête noire Columbia, where she reigned as Film Studies' Director of Undergraduate Studies for decades.

Annette literally taught me how to dance. Like Ginger Rogers to Fred Astaire, she also gave me sex appeal. For the first time in my adult life, I became comfortable with my body, and actually managed to smile when people talked to me. The ironic detachment that had been my MO began to recede and I valiantly tried to display genuineness over artifice.

The Education of Brainiac

The two Edwards, Annette Insdorf and me on
Elm Street in New Haven, 1977

By 1973 the direction of our relationship was a bit up in the air. Her omnipresent mother Cecile, herself an unforgettable character with a Polish accent and bouffant hairdo, was typically tight lipped, but Cecile's colleague Henry Hornik (Mrs. Insdorf was adjunct professor of French at Hunter College) thought we made a good pair. The fly in the ointment, of course, was that I had come out over the summer of 1973, so I had to get up the gumption to tell Annette. She could not have been more supportive, as she has been in so many ways of countless friends through the years.

If there is only one Annette Insdorf in my life, there have to be dozens of David Lapins in hers. She is loyal to the nth degree, and while relationships with her may wax and wane, there's never any doubt that Annechka, as I call her, is going to be there for you whenever you need her.

***

Coming out to Edward Feuerstein required more mettle. It actually required one or two gruesome walks around Grove Street Cemetery in New Haven on the afternoon of Halloween 1973. For reasons that now escape me, I thought the cemetery would prove an excellent venue for the conversation. Or maybe it was just because it was Halloween.

Since my move to New Haven, Edward regularly made trips to visit me and my new friends, most of whom were straight females, gay males, or what we now dub "questioning." I lived in the Hall of Graduate Studies, a gargantuan cloister and monastery that leaked everywhere. HGS as it was called was home to hundreds of graduate students who were lucky enough to live there over the disgusting Helen Hadley Hall, a 1950s structure that would win any competition for Yale's ugliest building. Lunches and dinners in the HGS dining hall raised my suspicion that maybe as much as half of the incoming students were gay. Some departments, like French, seemed in need of affirmative action for straight boys.

Coming out in that hothouse was not difficult. But coming out to specific friends like Edward was another story. We had known each other since we were twelve, We were basically family, and I certainly had no desire to tell any of the Lapins about my sexual orientation. Then there was also the question of Edward's predilections. I guessed he was gay, but what if he wasn't? A lot was on the line, and it took forever for me to get around to the subject at hand.

Finally, as we were almost set to leave the cemetery that we had entered an hour prior, I got the fraught sentence off my tongue: "Edward, I'm gay." Without dropping a beat he responded: "David, I'm gay and so is my brother." Check and checkmate! Twenty years would pass before I had the goods to one-up him: "Edward, I'm gay and so is Jonny."

I haven't mentioned that I am David Edward and Edward is Edward David. As we go through our lives as best friends, we still discover the oddest things about each other. I guess that's the stuff that makes life worth living.

Chapter 21
Hobbled

Coming out was not the same as having sex. Coming out, I convinced myself, was all about politics and truthfulness. As for the nub of the matter, I dithered on that score well into winter 1974. "David, less talk, more action" became the season's mantra, thanks to an English graduate student.

It wasn't as if I was looking for a life partner. I just had developed a narrow aesthetic that admitted few comers. Finally when I found Mr. Sorta Right, he turned out to be impotent! And to make matters worse, in an attempt to ingratiate himself to me, he listened one Saturday afternoon to all six hours of the Met's broadcast of Richard Wagner's *Götterdämmerung*. Who does that? He hadn't even heard *La bohème*. Not particularly strange to say, it was a big turnoff, and Mr. Right and I quickly separated.

The problem with girl or boy sex in New Haven is that it's a small town where everyone sooner or later knows your predilections and allergies. Around 1976 a rumor spread that the Club Baths was considering opening a branch in New Haven. I was absolutely horrified, not because of any aversion to the baths, but because I would know everyone in it.

Telling tales out of the bedroom was pretty much standard operating procedure in those days, and no sooner would I bid farewell to a trick—the floodgates opened after the Mr. Right debacle—than I was on the phone with someone detailing every aspect of what had just transpired. The post-coital conversation was at least as important as the sex itself, and I was hardly the only one in town playing both sports.

My first drink at a gay bar, the Pub, was a real sissy cocktail—Sloe Gin Fizz. The Pub was pretty much a pre-Stonewall milieu where leaning even slightly toward someone in one of the banquettes got you a slap on the wrist from the proprietor, who we nicknamed Morticia. Fortunately, a new bar opened in Spring 1974, and Partners became *the* place to go, not just for gays, but also Yalies looking to burnish their reputations as beautiful people. One night, a buddy of mine introduced me to an older guy with a mustache who looked slightly disheveled. It didn't take me long to realize that I was talking to the playwright Edward Albee. Only well-honed Yale cool prevented me from acting like a total klutz.

***

Reconciling all my boys and girls with political science required a delicate balance. Except for Morris McCain, I had not come out to anyone in the Department, and there was still more than a whiff of homophobia around Prospect Street. Fortunately, I found a mentor among the faculty who at least recognized whatever talents I had and actually did something to nurture them.

Charles Lindblom had trained as an economist, but his scholarship focused on connections between politics and markets. In 1974 he was asked to lead Yale's Institute for Social and Policy Studies, a think tank that facilitated interdisciplinary conversations around public policy. With the Watergate scandal coming to a head that summer, Lindblom organized a Project on the Future of American Institutions. The acronym POFADI didn't sit real well with folks (say it out loud three times fast), so the Project was renamed POADI—I guess the Future became an agnostic choice.

Lindblom, whose graduate course I had taken the prior spring (while screwing myself blind), asked me to become POADI's staff assistant, which I eagerly agreed to. I don't think I appreciated at the time what Lindblom's tutelage meant. He had developed a terrible reputation as a thesis advisor based on one or two failed efforts. Whatever the validity of that assessment, Lindblom was an absolutely brilliant thinker and, to my mind, the keenest minded professor in Political Science. I consider my decision not to have him direct my thesis as the worst mistake of my academic life. But Lindblom was more than thirty years older than me, and once again, my dread of older men played its foolish hand.

POADI sent me to Washington to interview members of the Senate and House Select Committees that investigated Nixon and his henchmen. We hosted on-campus forums with Senator Daniel Patrick Moynihan (who professed admiration for Lindblom's books), *The Washington Post's* Ben Bradlee (whose Yalie son Dino offended me by calling me "slender"), Hubert Humphrey (who I detested because of Vietnam), and Lesley Stahl, who had gained national prominence as one of the few women reporters on the Watergate beat. It was all heady stuff for a twenty-four year old, and I savored my new prominence in the Department.

***

David E. Lapin

Having served a term as Robert Dahl's teaching assistant for his lecture class *Democracy and Its Critics*, I decided in 1976 to put in an application to teach my own course through Yale's college seminar program. I submitted a proposal, *American Democracy and the Limits to Growth*, to one of Yale's residential colleges, Davenport, where I was a graduate fellow. Much to my surprise, the proposal was not only accepted; it received over 100 student applications.

As far as I recall, *Limits to Growth* and its sequel, the *Politics of Energy*, were the first energy and environmental policy courses offered through the Political Science Department. I gained several acolytes among the undergraduates, and by 1977, my future as a political scientist looked as bright as Jimmy Carter's young presidency. I had passed my Master of Philosophy exams (one of two with Distinction) and graduated to ABD (all but dissertation) status. If the world wasn't my oyster, the view was certainly looking up.

All I had to do was submit a dissertation prospectus and identify a thesis advisor. I might as well have tried climbing Kilimanjaro on one foot.

***

Douglas Rae had been a graduate student alongside my Queens College mentor Madi Adler at the University of Wisconsin. Having completed his own thesis on the political consequences of electoral law, Rae had recently been granted tenure at Yale. Lindblom invited Rae to join POADI, and I promptly became impressed by Doug's insightful observations. Though he still had some strands of his own at the time, Rae was no longhair—I once had to tell him that Pachelbel was the composer and *Canon* was his composition. Still, he seemed heads higher than his mediocre peers.

I had long conversations with two of my fellow graduate students, Jennifer Hochschild and Judy Gruber. Both were also seeking an advisor, and the Lindblom-Rae debate occupied center stage in our conversations. I take full responsibility for picking Rae over Lindblom; Jennifer and Judy did the same, and both went on to distinguished careers, though Judy's was tragically cut short by a fatal cancer. In short order, the Lapin-Rae combo proved to be the square peg and a round hole. Nothing about it clicked.

The semester I submitted my prospectus to Doug, he was on leave in Wassenaar, Holland. I dutifully mailed him the three page affair, and waited for a response. I marked time for six months. You would think that I would have gotten the message and moved on. But no, my penchant for passivity once again took hold and I awaited Rae's return to New Haven.

We set up a meeting in Fall 1977 and, yes, he had received the prospectus. The problem was that the most impactful comment came in the form of a rather large coffee stain on page one. He nonetheless approved it and formally agreed to become my advisor.

Whew. I was finally off and running—as I said, on one foot.

Chapter 22
Purgatory

Graduate students in the seventies were allotted two years to live on campus, and then they needed to find their own digs in New Haven. I had spent a couple of summers living off campus with Morris McCain, but by fall 1974, I needed to find my own space outside HGS and the blanketing security of Mother Yale.

The city then was no different than it is today. The only divide that matters is whether you're town or gown. Racial animosity ran high with an economically disenfranchised African American community scraping by in a city whose only big employers were Yale and the telephone company. Jobs were hard to come by and they didn't pay much if you got one.

Into that picture add the hapless students who lived in the netherworld between the Yale campus and the Hill, Dixwell and Dwight neighborhoods. A friend of mine had recently moved to a grand Victorian house on Dwight Street that could have been designed by Stanford White. It was owned by a bachelor named Walter Hald, who also owned the anachronistic stables and barn behind it and another large house around the corner on Elm Street. Mr. Hald let me know that the first floor apartment on Elm Street was available and I moved in that September with the *Québécois* Louis Allaire, an anthropologist-in-the-making, as my housemate.

All proved peaceful until Thanksgiving. I had decided to stay home for the holiday, instead of visiting my peripatetic parents who had recently fled New York for the bucolic exurbs of Berks County, Pennsylvania. I was watching the *Mary Tyler Moore Show* on my tiny black and white television when I heard this strange scraping noise coming from Allaire's bedroom (he was away). Seeking to investigate I entered Louis's bedroom and witnessed a would-be burglar about to jump through one of the windows. Mr. Hald had attached chicken wire mesh to all the windows and my rather young thief-in-training had already succeeded in removing that feeble impediment, hence the scraping sound.

Doing all I could to look macho, I folded my arms and attempted a pallid imitation of Mr. Clean. Just as he was about to leap, he caught sight of me, and turned tail toward Mr. Hald's stable. Being a do gooder and shaking in my shoes, I stumbled toward the telephone and called the police, who came over in about ten minutes.

That's when the real fun began. Seating me in the back of the patrol car, they whisked me off to a local dive bar on nearby Howe Street, where to my astonishment, they lined up all the patrons on the street for my inspection. Somehow, I heard the voice of my eighth grade tormentor Max reminding me, "You're dead." Did they really expect me out in the open to point a finger at a possible suspect? YES. Sanity prevailed and I respectfully declined the cops' kind invitation.

The Education of Brainiac

Partying on Elm Street, 1974

Two future holidays brought forth similar episodes. On Independence Day 1976 (the Bicentennial year), I was in Pennsylvania visiting my folks when another break-in proved successful. We had latches on all the windows that prevented anyone from opening them more than five or six inches. No problem! Shove a kid horizontally through the gap and get the child to open the front door for the adults. I lost my bicycle and my prized Sony open reel tape deck on that occasion. I did get a kick out of knowing that the burglars made off with my homemade recording of *Siegfried* with Jess Thomas and Birgit Nilsson; I wondered how far they got listening to *that*.

Next year, we lowered the latches so that the windows couldn't be raised more than three inches. It was a very hot and humid July but it did the trick. On Independence Day 1977 the thieves came with a ladder and burglarized the second floor apartment. As for me in apartment one, I got off unscathed save for a minor PTSD. That September, I fled my nightmare on Elm Street for the safe confines of a studio apartment at University Towers on York Street.

The sad part of this story, aside from burglary as a profession, was Yale's complicity in keeping stories like these out of the news as much as possible. The University had a vested interest in polishing its brand, and if that meant sacrificing a few students to hushed up crimes, so be it. At least in the seventies, guns were not the common currency that they would become in the nineties, when the undergraduate Christian Prince was killed with a bullet to his heart. It took that much to hold Yale accountable, as the University began a massive security effort to prevent yet another blemish to its damaged reputation.

***

While New Haven had its charms, the siren sounds of New York City regularly beckoned me on weekends. Once out of sheer boredom, Edward Turk and I decided to throw an impromptu party on a Friday night at Edward's apartment, also at University Towers. (Edward was on the fourth floor, I was on the tenth, and Annette was sandwiched somewhere in between. It made for a very nice communal lifestyle.) Much to our amazement, everyone we invited showed up. No one had anything else to do.

Taking what used to be the New Haven Railroad into Grand Central proved too tempting, and on many occasions, more of my comrades were to be found in New York than in New Haven. New York in those days had two principal attractions for me, sex and opera. It was a golden age for both. The city itself was falling apart, but that had scant impact on my nocturnal avocations.

In the seventies, the Met had a buzz. Coming off legendary general manager Rudolf Bing's twenty-two year tenure, the Company had recently hired a *wunderkind* named James

Levine to galvanize the orchestra. The repertoire also expanded post-Bing (as did the deficits), and newish operas like *Lulu*, *Death in Venice*, and *Dialogues of the Carmelites* were given compelling premieres. Perhaps most important, great singers like Jon Vickers, Marilyn Horne, Teresa Stratas, Montserrat Caballé and Renata Scotto were still in their prime. The house often sold out.

The wonder is how I afforded Met tickets on an impoverished graduate student's income. Beats me, but I got in somehow, often buying standee tickets and hoping to snag a vacant seat. I went with Ester Fuchs to see *Falstaff*, Georgette Gestely to see *Der Rosenkavalier*, and Edward Feuerstein to see *Salome*. It was Edward's first night at the opera, and he chortled annoyingly through the great Leonie Rysanek's Dance of the Seven Veils. No chortles the next time: Edward cried as Montserrat Caballé sang "Casta Diva" from *Norma*. For the next forty years, he and our mutual friend Alice Avrutin-Yellin—who earned early celebrity from a wicked rum punch at Yale—were regular Met subscribers, balcony, row one, and directly on the aisle to accommodate Edward's long legs.

***

Sometimes a night at the opera would extend into a night at the bars or baths. I never patronized the famous Continental Baths or the dingy Everard, where a fire once forced its patrons out on the sidewalks with only towels as apparel. But I did frequent Man's Country on West 15th Street and the Club Baths at First and First. Man's Country unfolded over multiple stories, and the challenge of walking up and down its stairs over four or five hours left me utterly exhausted. But it did have cages and even a full sized tractor trailer. It also let in students like me at a steep discount.

The Club was more popular. It stayed open until the AIDS epidemic got out of control. On my last night there around 1983 and with caution as my keynote, I paraded around one final time with the requisite towel, but also with white crew socks to prevent me from picking up whatever virus was promulgating the plague. If you've seen Armie Hammer in *Call Me by Your Name,* you'll know what those ridiculous socks looked like with Brainiac wearing them.

Besides the Baths, there were the clubs. My favorites were the Ice Palace on West 57th Street, the Crisco Disco in Chelsea, *Le Jardin* on West 43rd, *Les Mouches* on West 11th Avenue (where I attended the Up Against the Wall Anita Bryant Ball), and The Mineshaft in the Meatpacking district. The Mineshaft was by far the filthiest.

For my twenty-eighth birthday, my last Elm Street housemate John Treat took me to the Mineshaft. Dressed in leather and jeans, we arrived early, around 1 AM, and stayed until sunrise, though we'd hardly know that from the windowless setting. A clothes check was supposedly available, but John and I noted that most people just dropped their clothes on the floor. Whatever heights or depths of sexual expression you could imagine were showcased in various dedicated rooms, some of which we found too fetid to enter.

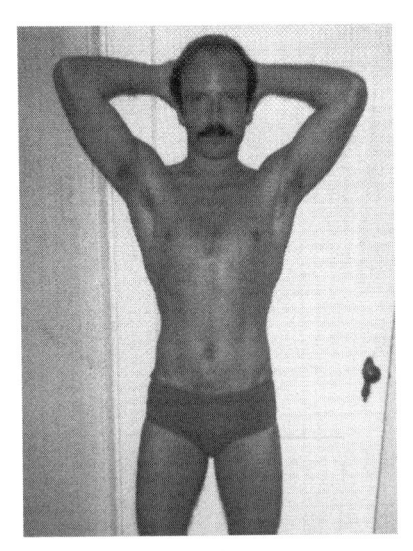

The Buff Years

The high (or low) point for me was entirely voyeuristic. Two totally naked and great looking guys, one black haired and the other blond, passed us in the dark like Greek satyrs. The blond was running from the black haired guy, but not with sufficient conviction. As he climbed up a cage, black haired guy caught up with him and proceeded to fist blond guy, as blond guy tried to escape by climbing higher up the cage. Both were also drugged on something or another.

I left thinking two things. First, that the Mineshaft could definitely use showers. And second, that I had seen enough. I had reached satyr satiety.

Chapter 23
Amantes

Making friends, even keeping some for life, is one of my talents. Making and keeping *amantes*, as I call them, has proven to be a wholly different affair. The cruel truth for Brainiac is that the hunt often proves more important than the capture. My romantic fixations typically zero in on those I can't have sex with, and those I do have sex with are usually gone in six weeks or under. Or they become friends for life.

In the eighties and early nineties I obsessed over Mr. X for seven years. Nothing could break the spell he had over me, not even sleeping with him a half dozen times while his girlfriend was away for a summer gig. We didn't have sex, and that's why the spell wasn't broken. It was David Lapin to a T. Before Mr. X there was Navy Man. He too had a steady girlfriend but that didn't stop me from getting him to go abroad with me. Same formula—mutual romantic attachments partially expressed, but no sex.

Looking back on these affairs, I now recognize how two combustible elements combined to produce this peculiar pattern. First was my inability to conceive of same sex relationships in everyday domestic terms. Recall that for me as a teenager, two individuals lived happily ever after; any roadmap for getting there was nonexistent. Second was coming to terms with AIDS. By the early eighties, gay sex was an ever more risky proposition. And no one knew what to do to reduce the risk—except not having sex at all. I opted for a middle of the road strategy. I would pursue straight guys. I only dimly intuited how foolhardy this approach was. And yet, it remains one plan of attack to this day.

***

As for earlier boyfriends, let me describe two. Both of course had girlfriends. Both were Yalies. And there, the similarities end. Andy Chen was the stud of Yale campus, generously having sex with boys and girls alike. He was a hunk by anyone's measure, more than amply endowed, and good looking to boot. One August, I met him at Partners, though he had been on my radar for months. He had long black hair and a jaunty, if slightly bow legged gait.

My night with Andy on Elm Street was almost a bust. I had never been a bottom and despite his best efforts, he wasn't making headway. Just when I thought all was lost, I unintentionally relaxed, and nature took its course. The next day, I spent hours in the University Towers swimming pool recuperating. It took about six months for that obsession to dim, though we continued to hook up for about a year.

Andy Chen

After Andy came John Bommer Murphy, a free spirit who would be a man apart in any setting, kind of Jean Genet without the thefts. John's girlfriend had a mustache. He often wore makeup. He was a budding visual artist, who also applied his aesthetic sensibility to the way he dressed and presented himself. He was timeless, and a photograph he took of himself in the seventies, now in my possession, could have been produced yesterday. He had golden locks and ruby lips. He was as beautiful as Andy was handsome. John and I stayed together for a few months before he took off for a semester abroad in Venice. We saw each other a couple of times on his return, but by then the flame inevitably burned low. On leaving Yale, he moved to California for graduate studies at Santa Barbara, and I never saw him again. Sad to say, John died of AIDS while in his twenties. I still keep his self-portrait behind my desk.

A Self-Portrait of John

***

Standard Brainiac procedure in the eighties allowed for the occasional romantic liaison. The longest lasting was with a Harvard professor who I had met during my year at Cornell on one of my trips to Boston. I found him reasonably attractive, and I guess he felt the same way about me. We may have been together off and on for a few years, though when it ended definitively, I could not tell you. There were never any sparks to the relationship, as I gather you can discern from the last couple of sentences. But he was my intellectual equal, and we got along okay, despite his annoying precedent for nicknaming me Grumpy. This kind of summarizes it—friendly with if's, and's and but's. He eventually found a new boyfriend, and I was just fine with that.

The early eighties were probably the low water mark as far as my interest in girls was concerned. At Yale, I had the occasional coed with a crush on me. There were no hard and fast rules back then about relationships with one's students, but I never had sex with anyone I taught. In 1979, I moved to Ithaca to accept a position in the Cornell Government Department. For academia, it was friendly enough, perhaps too friendly as far as a couple of women professors were concerned.

I did seriously contemplate marrying a woman around 1987. But by the 1990s, a clear convention ruled over my personal life. I fended off available females, while pursuing unattainable males. Some might say that was queer. I would just say, that was me.

Chapter 24
Solo in Ithaca

My final years in New Haven consisted of one abortive attempt after another to get the dissertation underway. My idea was to write something called *The Doctrine Of Growth in American Democracy*, and it would demonstrate how democratic viability depended on economic growth.

One hurdle to clear was whether this was going to be an empirical, data driven enterprise, or a theoretical inquiry. My inclination was to emphasize the latter. No one to this day, so far as I know, has figured out what democratic theory is, so that presented one stumbling block. In the 1950s Robert Dahl had written a slim, widely acclaimed treatise called *A Preface to Democratic Theory*, and that's about as far as he ever got. A second impediment was my stubborn even irrational resistance to taking empirical data seriously. I can see now how this bias jeopardized my political science bona fides, but so be it. I was stuck with who I was, and marrying data (reality) to theory (neat systems quite separate from reality) just wasn't my thing.

I also spent more and more time reading, rather than writing. Everything seemed relevant, from Brian Barry's *Political Argument* to John Rawls' *A Theory of Justice* to E.F.

Schumacher's *Small is Beautiful*. At some point, you have to give it a rest, but I had a hard time figuring out when that was. Endless conversations with colleagues only further muddied the waters.

Add to this quagmire the fact that I was also teaching and looking for a full-time position. The Carter years of the late seventies weren't good for job hunters. Despite this, in 1978, I began to interview and a few places showed interest. I traveled to Amherst and Hampshire Colleges to make presentations. I showed up at conventions of The American Political Science Association, and snagged a meeting with a recruiter from The University of Colorado at Boulder, only to be told by the douchebag that he was just interested in my topic, not me.

Finally I got a real offer from a place I never heard of, The College of Charleston in South Carolina. I really liked the department chair, the students I met and the urban milieu. The fly in the ointment was that I would be required to teach eight courses over two semesters, and I knew that would doom any chance I had for finishing my thesis.

The evening before my departure for Cornell
with Wally Jaffe and Ralph Vitello

As spring 1979 was drawing to a close, two offers came out of the blue. I chose Cornell over Columbia because Cornell offered more money and required less teaching. It was a no brainer. Both were one year positions, but hey it was a start. One of my craziest and most brilliant friends, Ralph Vitello, and I traveled to Ithaca and I signed a lease for an apartment over a dentist's office on Dryden Road in Collegetown. Only later would I learn that my water supply all but shut down once daily drilling commenced downstairs.

My post-New Haven life was finally taking shape.

***

Ithaca is a place you either love or hate. When I visited for my interview in May, the sky was blue and the surrounding hills were verdant. It looked terrific.

When I returned in September, clouds had covered the hills, and a depressing grey blanket had settled over the town. The clouds and the grey stayed around until the following May. As a city boy, I just couldn't get used to rural New York, and daily smells from the nearby pig farm did nothing to encourage any accommodation to my new habitat.

I did add to my teaching portfolio by giving Cornell's undergraduate course on Congress. I also repeated my *Energy* and *Limits to Growth* classes, and found the Cornell kids overall as gifted as the Yalies I had left behind. The problem wasn't the students or the professors. I actually liked most of them. The trouble was I didn't have the network of friends that had made New Haven bearable.

Ithaca's gay social life was pretty much nonexistent, or at least what I discovered of it. I visited the only gay bar once in September and once in May. Both times I found myself attracted to the same guy, so on visit number two, we hooked up. Everybody has a tic; his was somnambulism. He disappeared from the bedroom in the middle of the night and I found him the next morning sleeping on the living room floor. He swore he had no recollection of how he wound up there and I believed him.

My other social high point was going out with a colleague to the Ramada Inn for square dance lessons. We were the only ones who showed up, so the lessons were canceled. After that desperate experience, I attempted getting drunk on Dewar's in the privacy of my apartment. I decided I had no taste for Scotch, and so that experiment also ended in failure.

At twenty nine, I was as physically attractive as I was ever going to be, at least in my estimation, but my social life had collapsed into a black hole. I tried reviving a relationship I had begun before leaving New Haven, but he was having none of it. My long distance phone bill topped a hundred dollars a month—a lot of money on my 1979 salary—but it was my only lifesaver. I knew by December that I had to get out of town for good.

I could have tried harder to fit in. I could have taken up skiing or gone back to ice skating, a sport I started in New Haven that won me the heart of a national amateur champion. But my heart just wasn't in it. I yearned for the company of friends, and that meant deciding which friends and which city would form the next chapter in Brainiac's life.

***

I chose Boston over New York. San Diego, which I had never visited, came in a distant third. It was a flippant choice, the kind you make because you're still in your twenties and anything seems possible. Not much thought went into it. I didn't have a job lined up anywhere. But Boston won out, and the decision changed my life. It also may have saved it, given the plague that was beginning to settle over New York.

I packed my worldly belongings on Memorial Day weekend 1980 and headed east, where I would reunite with my old pal Edward Turk. Everything I owned was in the U-Haul truck with one exception—my prized pornography collection. I was mortally afraid of getting into an accident and having nudie magazines flying all over Interstate 90. So I carefully packed them, stapled the parcel multiple times, and walked my booty to the post office. "Media mail rate, please," I informed the postal worker, mindful of getting a discounted price. Without forewarning, she grabbed the parcel from my hands and started ripping out the staples! In near panic, I thought to myself, "How does she know?"

I grabbed the package back and blurted out something like, "Oh, it doesn't have to go media rate." She gently tugged it back in her direction. "Oh, that's okay, dear. I don't have to see it. I just don't like staples." At which point she continued to remove and replace them with a big, fat swath of tape.

If my heart stopped beating, I wouldn't have known it. I was too traumatized and may have sworn at that point never to buy another dirty magazine again. And of course, I didn't, but only because the world of VHS video was just around the corner.

Chapter 25
Raunchy Roommates

If Ithaca offered a dearth of social possibilities, Boston provided a surfeit, many just plainly bizarre thanks to my newest roommate. I met Peter Beverage in early April while apartment hunting in Boston. Edward Turk had spied a classified in *The Boston Phoenix* for a GWM seeking the same in a roommate. The prime attraction, according to Edward, was that the apartment was located in Bay Village, one of Boston's oldest and smallest neighborhoods. It was also a very gay place in 1980, and even its straight residents often affectionately referred to it as Gay Village.

When I first met Peter, he was dressed in a suit and tie as befitted his position as a trainer-educator at Bank of Boston. When he met me to give me the keys on the Friday afternoon I arrived, he was similarly attired. He then went back to the bank, as Edward helped me to unload the U-Haul.

Peter and I had agreed to the following arrangement. He would occupy the basement level of the duplex apartment, which had the only bedroom, and pay $200 toward the rent. I would occupy the open living space on the first floor, which also contained a galley kitchen and bathroom. In consideration of my lack of privacy, I would pay $160. That suited me just fine, as my primary income at the time was unemployment compensation, thanks to the State of New York.

That first evening, Peter returned from work, went downstairs to his quarters, dropped the suit, and returned shortly in full S&M leather regalia, with chains alongside color-coded handkerchiefs to identify various fetishes. I wish I could remember all of them, but the only one that comes to mind as I write this is yellow.

Despite my shock & awe, I remained composed and did a pretty good job of projecting nonchalance. That was all to the good, because the kinks had just begun. Having driven all day from Ithaca, I was exhausted and decided to try falling asleep on the incredibly uncomfortable green sleeper sofa that Peter generously provided. Peter said good evening and left for points unknown.

Several hours passed when I was awakened by noises at the apartment entrance. It must have been about two in the morning. Peter had returned with not one, not two, but THREE men he had picked up at Boston's notorious Combat Zone bar, Playland—charming name for the raunchiest bar in town.

All four made their way downstairs where the fun was about to begin. I succeeded in tuning out most of the slurps and slaps; what I couldn't ignore was our guests' need to use the bathroom, not just for peeing, God forbid, but for puking from too much beer. Peter was very solicitous, and guided them up the stairs, each in his turn. It was all very civil, and by 5 AM, the three had departed, presumably for their respective home torture chambers. Peter went back to sleep, as did I—I guess—at some point.

It was a night to remember, but two nights later proved even more stimulating. Peter told me that I had replaced Jean Masse, his lover, with whom he had recently broken up. But now they were having second thoughts. Would I mind, for a further concession on the rent, if Jean moved back in? Sure, I said, mindful of my tight budget.

Thus I found myself in cohabitation with two S&M queens. They basically lived in the basement, but would occasionally come up to use the kitchen—usually to reheat leftover pizzas—and relieve themselves in the men's room. At some point, if I didn't find myself yearning for the odors of the pig farm in Ithaca, at least I began to recall them with a fondness that was all but unthinkable less than a month prior.

Jean was totally obnoxious. He made one play for me, which went nowhere, and then we settled into a wary détente. I never knew from one night to the next whether he would be fighting with Peter, screwing with Peter, crying and breaking up with Peter, or crying and getting back together with Peter. It all became a blur like the memory of a bad movie. Edward and I maliciously called him the *Ungeheuer* (German for monster) and for once a moniker seemed utterly apt.

***

The wonder of it all is that, in this insane asylum, I actually finished my dissertation by December. Edward Turk is a fantastic reader, and he helped me to refashion my argument by turning it one-hundred eighty degrees. I made a cogent case that democratic systems are viable under a wide spectrum of economic growth rates. I also argued that while there is no intrinsic value to zero growth, rates could be guided lower if necessary to accommodate multiple environmental and social problems arising from growth itself.

Not to my surprise, *No-Growth Democracy: A Theoretical Inquiry into the Viability of Democratic Systems in the Absence of Economic Growth* hit a firewall of criticism. How could I be against economic growth? I wasn't. Why hadn't I been more empirical? That was a given. Why couldn't I write better? I'll leave that criticism to the readers of this memoir for their consideration. My style really hasn't changed much in decades.

The funniest response was from my advisor, Douglas Rae, who opined that the dissertation was fine, but I should have spent more time polishing my case. There in a nutshell lies the folly of graduate studies. Having spent four years under his tutelage, it would really be beneficial to spend one more year spinning my intellectual wheels. No thank you, said I to Doug. In any event, my doctorate had been secured.

I knew I had burned my bridge but I was happy to do it. I actually had one final interview that winter at Harvard. I placed my best foot forward, but I knew my chances were slim. And with that, I left higher education for good. I'm sure to some it will always seem like sour grapes, but I've never been more convinced of having made the right move in my life.

***

As for Peter and Jean, they broke up for good and Peter, who was about five feet five inches tall, found a new boyfriend, also named Peter, who was at most four feet eleven inches tall. (The *Ungeheuer* was about six-foot one.) Once they hooked up, Peter Beverage decided to move out. I wish I could say that Peter and Peter's Peter lived happily ever after. But as was too often the case by the mid-eighties, Peter and Jean died of AIDS. Bay Village was becoming a ghost town, and I began feeling a world collapsing around me.

Chapter 26
"A Great Place"

There was one offshoot to my life in academe. Annette Insdorf had ignited my interest in film, and I became especially intrigued by the works of the Italian director Bernardo Bertolucci. With Annette's support, I crafted a course called *Politics and Film*, which I gave at Yale in the summer of 1979. The following year, my first in Boston, I returned to New Haven on Wednesdays to give a course on Bertolucci and Italian cinema. With my dissertation nearing completion, I also secured an agreement from an editor named Warren French to publish my proposed book on Bertolucci. French had been responsible for Annette's study of François Truffaut and while there was little money in the deal, it did open a new road outside mainstream political science for me to explore.

Bertolucci was best known for *Last Tango in Paris* with Marlon Brando. But the film that really hit me in the gut was *The Conformist* with Jean-Louis Trintignant. Based on a novel by Alberto Moravia, the film, through brilliant, disjointed narrative techniques, explored political and sexual repression in Mussolini's Italy. Bertolucci would go on to win the Oscars for Best Director and Best Picture for his magnum opus, *The Last Emperor,* in 1987. Unfortunately, by then, my publisher had long since gone belly up, and the market for book-length film director studies had shrunk substantially. I tried peddling the book concept for a couple of years, and did publish an article on Bertolucci in *Literature/Film Quarterly*. But the handwriting was on the wall: without the financial backstops of an academic position, I simply did not have the time or the money to complete the project. This failure nags at me to this day.

***

"It's a great place. You ought to get to know it better, even if you don't get the job." The comments came from John Pearson, a dashing fifty-something trust officer from Pawhuska, Oklahoma, who was Edward Turk's boyfriend in 1981. I had recently spied a tiny advertisement in *The Boston Globe* for the position of registrar at the Community Music Center of Boston. I wasn't even sure what a registrar was or did. But the twenty-hour a week job would give me time to continue working on Bertolucci, or so I thought. John had been involved as a trustee at the Music Center, and with his endorsement, I got the job in time for the opening of the school year in September 1981, fifteen full months after my move to Boston. I would remain at the Music Center for thirty-six years.

Started in 1910 as two separate settlement schools, the Music Center had touched the lives of generations of Bostonians, especially recent immigrants to America for whom music education was perceived as a ladder toward middle class respectability. I was instinctively attracted to the place for its grassroots feel. No government mandate willed it into existence. The good works of patrons and musicians alone ensured its continued success or failure. I felt that I had come face to face with the spirit of volunteerism that Alexis de Tocqueville identified as the essence of *Democracy in America*. For the first time in my life, politics and music fused in a singular way

The Education of Brainiac

that appealed to my brain, my heart and my soul. I guess you could say I was falling in love.

The Music Center was headed by an oversized singer named Michael Garroway, the son of the *Today Show's* first host, Dave Garroway. Michael sat me at my desk in the front office my first day on the job and told me to record five dollar registration fees from any students who came to register. These were my first and last marching orders. That first week, I took five dollars from about one hundred families and individuals, including the retired postal worker Edgar Troncoso. Edgar was especially memorable because he told me he aspired to sing Donizetti's "Una furtiva lagrima"—a favorite of tenors from Caruso to Pavarotti—at the next student recital. I came home each evening exhausted, but also elated at my good fortune in finding a workplace with a motley cast of characters whom I instantly identified with.

At the beginning of week two, the annual faculty meeting was scheduled, and Michael introduced me to all the members. I was having a jolly good time until the pianist Frederic Davis came up to me and asked for his teaching schedule. Ditto for the garlic-saturated violinist Izidorius Vasyliunas. It only dawned on me then—and I know that this strains credulity—that the registrar didn't simply receive tuition. I also was responsible for pairing hundreds of kids and adults with their teachers! Fortunately, a high school aide named Martha came to my rescue. Martha had worked in the spring with my predecessor, who had been fired for embezzling small change—the only kind possible at the Center. She showed me how to assign students to teachers (the task that Michael had failed to mention), and by the first day of classes, everyone had been accommodated. It was baptism by fire, and I learned never again to let my guard down. Henceforth, I would do what I still do best, that is, stay on top of things before you find yourself screwed. It's a formula I would commend to any boss or manager to this day.

***

With Peter Beverage's departure from Bay Village, I was in desperate need of a new housemate. Fortuitously, the Music Center was only a few blocks from my apartment, so I had no desire to leave it. Edward had been living on Charles Street on Beacon Hill. His apartment was unique. The loft ceiling was so high that precipitation regularly formed under the skylight and fell as rain droplets on the plants and furnishings below. It was also freezing since the landlord ripped out the steam radiators and replaced them with insufficient electric baseboard heaters. The cost of the heating had also shifted from landlord to tenant. Feeling both cold and financially pinched, Edward decided to leave Charles Street and move in with me. That was in 1981, and he didn't leave until 2013.

Whenever some curious being asks me why I never married, I remind them of two things. First, I worked side by side at the Music Center with a colleague named Lucy Joan Sollogub for thirty-six years, longer—Lucy and I are fond of saying—than most marriages last. And second, I lived with Edward Turk in Bay Village for almost as long.

With Edward Turk at 31 Winchester Street, 1985

Working with Lucy was a constant pleasure. But how Edward and I survived for so long without killing each other is yet another chapter in Brainiac's tale.

Chapter 27
Roller Coasters

It took about six months for the rose to lose its bloom at the Music Center. Ditto for living with Edward, though that time period was more like six days.

***

On our first meeting in New Haven, Edward not only did not like me, he actually thought I was trying to expose him as intellectually weak and inferior. I for my part barely gave him a second thought. He was four years older than me, out of my league, and already a member of the Yale faculty. A seventeenth century scholar of Baroque French fiction making, Turk somehow construed my sophomoric badinage with him as thinly veiled threats to his super-fragile ego. He was, in short, paranoid and delusional.

Despite his crackpot thinking, I grew to like Edward who I found smart, stimulating and funny. He was a mass of neuroses, but so was I, and we both shared the same self-perceived indignity of having gone to The City University of New York, in his case Brooklyn College. If we weren't peas in a pod, we had enough in common to form a nascent friendship.

The trick was to ignore reality and converse as characters other than ourselves. Edward became Judy Garland and I was the pre-Johnny Carson *Tonight Show* host Jack Paar interviewing Judy. Edward had grown up idolizing Garland—he must have been one of the few teens who watched her Sunday night television show over the horse opera *Bonanza*—and he had absorbed all of Judy's mannerisms and ticks. As the cliché goes, he WAS Judy Garland, and I was happy to play her straight man Paar if it meant ironing out the emotional wrinkles that got in the way of us having good times together.

Edward and I also shared the trauma of losing hair at an early age. By the time I first encountered him in 1973, Edward was completely bald, though he tried to hide the obvious with a combover. I still had a mop, but I was obsessed at keeping it combed just right because the great recession had already started. Moaning over our mutual hair loss became a chronic plaint.

In 1978, Edward had surgery for ulcerative colitis. He had accepted an appointment to MIT's Humanities Department the prior year, and the stress of building a career in a new city set off an inflammation that nearly killed him. The surgeons performed a colectomy—removal of the colon—and cured him thereby of colitis. It saved his life more than once, because in leaving him with a six centimeter stump for a rectum, Edward had to abandon his time-honored role as a bottom. No one in 1978 could have foreseen just how serendipitous this development was as AIDS would expand throughout Boston and the nation in the nineteen eighties.

***

By the early eighties, the Music Center had one big problem: losing money. As a nonprofit, the school wasn't designed to make money, but it didn't have to operate as if losing it was the goal. And that's precisely how it functioned. Well-healed trustees led by Philip K. Allen, the board chair, had grown accustomed to making up for deficits with their own year end giving. But even that wasn't enough, and by the time I came on the scene, we owed money to just about any bank that would lend it. Even worse, our landlord, the Boston Center for the Arts (BCA), reneged on a deal to pay back a quarter of a million dollars in leasehold improvements. Apparently those betterments didn't include a new roof because, among its other charms, the Pennock Building where we were housed leaked so badly that one dank teaching studio had been rendered permanently unusable.

The BCA was run by a beloved rogue with a Dickensian name, Royal Cloyd. Royal's principal skill was schmoozing gullible funders. An erstwhile Unitarian, he had convinced the City in 1971 that Boston needed an arts complex, and the Boston Center for the Arts was founded in a derelict bunch of buildings that had once housed the Boston Flower Exchange. Rumor had it that monies meant for the BCA would wind up in Mexico paying for Royal's winter getaways. I was once told that the Music Center's security system had been installed explicitly to prevent a relative of Royal's with a nasty addiction from stealing instruments—or anything else for that matter—that could be pawned quickly on nearby Washington Street.

By 1981, Royal's wayward governance style was old news, and the foundation spigot that was the principal source of BCA support for a decade had largely run dry. This only aggravated the Music Center's financial distress as donors became increasingly wary of giving to any BCA-housed organization. Boston Ballet was similarly hobbled. The Music Center in effect had become collateral damage.

But our wounds were also self-inflicted. Michael had been appointed executive director in 1975. He came to the position with two excellent ideas, both of which were innovative and integral to the Music Center's long-run viability. The first was to hire music therapists to work with individuals with special needs. The second was to bring artist-educators into the public schools to supplement the work of the system's own music teachers. Both programs became national models, and they continue to prosper to this day.

Unfortunately, Garroway hadn't a clue how to stanch the Center's fiscal bleeding. A singer by training, he would absent himself for days at a time to work with impresario Sarah Caldwell—his soulmate in losing money—and others on opera productions while the Music Center was left drifting. By May 1982, I concluded that another year like the last was impossible. And, in fact, all hell did brake loose that December.

***

While working at the Music Center was like riding a roller coaster, living with Edward was strictly downhill. Almost immediately, we fought tooth and nail. Edward regretted his move from day one, and I wasn't far behind. The miracle is that we survived together for thirty-two years. I would not have placed a dime on that prospect in 1981.

The first order of business was getting Edward's oversized furniture into the apartment. He had an enormous mahogany desk that he inherited from his grandfather. The problem was that there was no way it was going to get into Edward's basement quarters. And so we decided to accommodate the grandfather's desk on my floor, a mighty concession, I thought.

Then there was his blue and white crushed-velvet sofa, an aesthetic legacy from New Haven. No one but Edward loved it. (Well, not quite. Years later, we decided to get rid of the couch, and the Music Center's registrar at the time, Tor Snyder, thought he could use it for his apartment. He moved it with a friend to his place, where his wife took one look at it, and had it immediately removed to the curb for the next garbage pickup.) It, too, wound up on my ever shrinking floorspace.

Edward settled into his basement quarters, which he sarcastically dubbed the Hovel, and began whining about lack of sunlight. Then there wasn't enough heat. It went on and on. I became increasingly defensive and testy. I also had to tolerate a stream of nocturnal visitors, though nothing on the Peter Beverage order of magnitude.

Then there was the filth. I had observed Edward's domestic disorder in New Haven and Boston. But I just wasn't prepared to live in it. We were like *The Odd Couple's* Felix Unger and Oscar Madison without the comedy; at least it didn't seem funny at the time. We fought so badly that he thought I had come unhinged while I thought he was completely deranged. I even consulted with his future husband, Philip Cobb, on the possibility of institutionalization. Philip, whom Edward had known since New Haven and who was too smart to let Edward live with *him*, took the suggestion under advisement.

There was a comical side to our situation. While we yelled to our hearts' content in the Hovel, we tried restraining our voices on the first floor, in consideration of our upstairs neighbor, Dottie DeMont. Dottie was a "working gal," as she called herself. Dottie controlled the house thermostat, so we didn't want to get on her bad side. A devotee of cigarettes and rye whiskey, she rivaled Edward's incompetence as a chef, and the only food she seemed capable of cooking was a baked potato.

We lived in daily dread of offending Dottie with our fights. And we did get a phone call one day. Apparently she hated Judy Garland as much as Edward loved her. We had been playing the movie *Easter Parade*, not very loudly I thought, but the number "A Fella with an Umbrella" put her over the top. It was the only time she yelled at us to keep it down. And yet, she suffered in silence through so many other lost opportunities!

Chapter 28
Game On

As with airplane flights, I used to keep regular count of the number of people I had sex with. Both tallies posed methodological quandaries. Did connecting flights qualify as singular or plural? Did Bill Clinton's rules apply or should one utilize more liberal standards? Whatever judgment was rendered, I simply lost count at some stage of both planes and persons, though it's safe to say I never aspired to platinum status in any frequent flier program.

I've known guys who can only determine their partner totals through statistical inference based on years, weeks, estimated frequency per week, etc. Their mates number in the thousands. I never attained—nor did I aspire to—those Olympian heights, and my overall figure is still below a hundred. I did once have sex at the Club Baths with more persons simultaneously than I care to admit, but that was an exception and simply for the record book.

One thing that annoyed me about the baths was their gender exclusivity. On very rare occasion a woman might sneak in but that was generally frowned upon. Toward the end of the baths era in New York, the Continental refashioned its image and became Plato's Retreat, open to straight couples and lesbians but not gay males. That experiment was just as irksome. The Retreat closed for good in 1985, along with all the city's remaining bathhouses, thanks to New York's mayor, Ed Koch, who so far as I know never had sex with anyone.

Boston had a few baths and dirty movie houses, but I never went to any of them. Somehow Puritan legacy robbed Beantown of New York excess, and Boston nightlife seemed downright genteel to me after the Big Apple. Yes, there was the Fens, but even that was milquetoast compared with Central Park's Rambles. One true story from the Fens, courtesy of a friend who stumbled one night onto a totally naked guy roped to a tree. "Excuse me, sir," naked man opined. "My master's gone and left me here. Would you be so kind as to untie me?"

***

My randiest day's were definitely behind me by 1985. Work at the Music Center had taken over my waking hours and I simply did not have the time or energy to wander around at 1 AM looking for hookups. The "fruit loop" was only several blocks from Bay Village, around the Park Square Building at Arlington Street. But that was mainly older guys picking up hustlers. And then there was the nasty business of not knowing what was safe and what was deadly. That definitely placed the cork on flighty sex for me.

In the late 1970s, an epidemic of hepatitis struck the East Coast, and straight and gay Yalies were turning yellow overnight. I got used to regular trips to the infirmary to visit friends, whose bodies were permanently compromised by the disease. This experience left me with a healthy dose of paranoia when it came to sex (it was widely thought that hepatitis was communicated through contaminated oysters or sex) and I regularly went to see my doctor for gamma globulin shots—a prophylactic against the disease. By the time HIV came on the scene, I had already taken measures to restrict my repertoire, even if we didn't know exactly which acts were deadliest.

Humans are a resilient species and it amazes me to this day how creative sexual activity became in the last decades of the twentieth century. The more knowledge we gained about HIV, the more flexible we became until phone sex became as popular as the full Monty. Veterans of the 1990s will never think of the word "moderator" without thinking of phone sex. Whole new worlds like "chat rooms" seemed to spring up overnight. And phone bills, for some, skyrocketed through the roof.

I consider myself fortunate in the extreme that no one in my closest circle of friends died from HIV. Still, ten of my Bay Village neighbors succumbed. Twenty one of my Yale-New Haven buddies lost their lives. And eleven Boston acquaintances perished. I'm sure there are many more. Like most survivors, I feel guilty that I endured. But I'm also grateful that I pulled through. Dying young may appeal to some Romantics. But living a full life has had infinitely more pizzazz for me.

The Music Center also lost students and faculty members to AIDS. It was heartbreaking to see a six-year old and know that she was doomed. The same went for a fantastic percussion teacher. I would observe adult students in the hallways whose conditions visibly deteriorated from one week to the next. To its credit, the Board of Directors had made a commitment to reaching out to persons with HIV who couldn't come in for lessons, and we sent music therapists to the nearby Boston Living Center for several years.

***

In the early eighties the Music Center had its own life threatening crises to confront and by 1982, it had basically run out of steam (translate: money). The foundations that supported us were loathe to throw good dollars after bad, and meeting payrolls had become a twice monthly nightmare. Enter into this picture a wise woman named Joan Diver. Joan was executive director of the Hyams Foundation, one of our leading supporters. A former resident of the South End where the Music Center was located—her family would be profiled in Anthony Lukas's landmark 1985 account of Boston school desegregation, *Common Ground*—Diver made a grant to fund a task force that would investigate all aspects of the Music Center's operation.

Michael Garroway couldn't have been thrilled with this turn of events, but he had no other option. The board hired a firm, Technical Development Corporation, to staff the task force, and by Christmas 1982, a man two years my senior named Stephen J. Morgan was working with us as our principal consultant.

Like me, Steve had made the journey from a focus on energy conservation to nonprofit management. Hired by TDC to help nonprofits with their energy use, he quickly discovered that a whole array of needs often had to be addressed as well. As an undergraduate at Harvard, Steve had been the straight dorm-mate at Winthrop House of Andrew Tobias, the financial columnist who penned a gay memoir, *The Best Little Boy in the World*.

Steve organized committees on programs, community relations, development, management—I'm probably forgetting some. A keen observer, he quickly determined that the Music Center had no future with Michael at its head. For the next three months, that subtext played out within the workings of the various committees, as everyone knew what the endgame was, except perhaps Garroway himself.

Two officers at that time needed to be brought around. One was the new president, Joan S. Rice, a trust officer by profession who needed little convincing. The other was the treasurer Lincoln B. Hansel, an eccentric Yankee by anyone's reckoning whose old money came from the whaling trades of the early 1800s. Lincoln likened himself to a pirate. He also had a penchant for gambling on horses and Broadway shows, and had scored big time with *Fiddler on the Roof*.

Hansel had a big heart, and it mustn't have been easy for him to put the Music Center's interests over Michael's. Maybe he intuited that the best thing for Michael was an honorable exit. I'm not sure who delivered the news, but in February 1983, Garroway was eased out of office and I was named interim executive director.

***

It was Game On for me and the Music Center from that point forward. I worked my tail off to keep us afloat, and only a gentleman's agreement with our loan officer at State Street Bank kept us from sinking. But as each week unfolded, new confidence in me and the school grew, and by August 1983 Joan Rice and Lincoln Hansel asked me to become executive director. I wouldn't have said no in a million years. I dashed off my letter of acceptance and immediately left on a two-legged flight for a week of Montezuma's revenge in Acapulco, Mexico.

Acapulco, 1983

Chapter 29
Who I Am

The great thing about the Music Center are the people. They remain the oddest assortment of characters I've ever encountered. There was Monty McGargel, also known as BJ. Monty had multiple personalities and we'd never know who he'd be when he visited us to practice piano—brilliantly, I might add, if as wayward as BJ himself. He was regularly in touch with the moon through his boombox.

One day we were expecting a visit from two Church Home Society ladies who were contemplating supporting us. Monty by chance was in residence playing piano a la McGargel. He was incapable of putting together two cogent sentences, and I advised the ladies of such. Imagine when I opened the door to his practice studio to introduce them. I told him why they were there and for the first and only time in my presence, he projected total lucidity. "You got a great place here," said Monty to the Church ladies. "You really should consider supporting it."

Then there was Rosie Blindell, one of Boston's oldest madams with a rap sheet dating back to the 1930s. Rosie fashioned herself a coloratura soprano on the order of the French diva Lily Pons. "Yeah, I sing just like Lily Pons, honey," she told me before proceeding to make sounds like a goat choking to death. One day, Rosie came to me with a check for ten-thousand dollars. "Yeah, it's a gift honey, for all you do for the children." I was humbled—until she sued us some years later for failing to promote her career as a coloratura. We won that case, since her tax filings listed the gift as a charitable deduction, not tuition toward career furtherance.

The head of our public school outreach efforts was a German expatriate named Elsbeth Meuth. Elsbeth, I discovered, had a second career in addition to administration and teaching; she was a strip tease artist in Boston's Combat Zone. On making this discovery, I summoned Elsbeth to my office. "I want to support you, Els, but if any board member or school principal finds out about your stripping, there's not much that I can do to keep you from getting fired." "Ja, I see what you mean," she responded, "let me think this over." Two days later Elsbeth returned to tell me that she had decided to retire from her evening vocation, but not before recruiting one of her regular clients to become a Music Center trustee.

My first faculty meeting as executive director with Elsbeth Meuth on my right. Calvin Herst is on Elsbeth's right.

Perhaps the most memorable figure was our building custodian, Anthony DiSantis. Like BJ/Monty, Tony had multiple identities, but in his case they were designed to thwart the IRS from catching up with his chronic tax delinquency. I was constantly in touch with Treasury Department agents trying to collect Tony's back taxes. I finally convinced them it was a losing game, and they gave up their pursuit. Tony was always in debt to the Music Center as well, since he would barely wait till payday to request an advance on his next check.

Tony had a soft spot for women, most of them, and I was repeatedly doing damage control over his insufferably lewd advances. Once he decided to go on vacation to Hyannis on Cape Cod. I joked with him on his carnal pursuits and said crassly he was heading for Hi-Anus. Well, apparently he surmised that that was the proper pronunciation, because for the next few weeks he told everyone in earshot that he would be vacationing in Hi-Anus. When the Music Center moved in 1990 to its fresh facility, Tony resigned because the new place was too clean. He just couldn't take the lack of filth.

***

Life at the Music Center was incredibly fulfilling, but it couldn't make up for the void in my life that I felt another person might fill, man or woman, I didn't care. Most of this yearning was fantasy. I don't think I was ever programmed for domestic life. Still, though I knew I was doing good works professionally, there was definitely something missing. I just didn't have a clue what that was.

My charity résumé was polished weekly via volunteer duty at the Episcopal Church of the Advent on Beacon Hill. A friend had been attending services there for a while, and he also volunteered for the Tuesday community dinners. Without much thought, he asked whether I would join him as a server at the dinners, and without much thought, I agreed.

I helped with the dinners for almost a year without even conceiving of attending services. I wasn't a Jew for Jesus. I don't think I considered myself anything at that point. And then, one evening, I had a moment that could only be called desolate. I was in the garden outside Moseley Hall where our guests were about to be served. An aridness descended over me like a cloak, and for an instant, I felt naked of meaning or significance. I was completely and utterly emptied. As quickly as it arrived, the moment passed. I went back in, served the guests, and didn't think much more about what had just happened.

A week or two passed, and I flew to Fort Lauderdale on vacation, where I would hook up with my Advent friend. I knew what I would tell him, though I hadn't rehearsed or prepared for the big moment in any way. He met me at the baggage area and I immediately blurted, "I'm going to see Father Cranston for spiritual counseling." The Reverend John A. Cranston, or JAC, was the Advent's senior curate, and he also helped out at the community dinners. He was as eccentric in his own manner as Monty McGargel or Rosie Blindell. He was also lots of fun to be around. For the first time since my teenage years, I felt I could trust an older man.

Mind you, I wasn't prepared to confess Jesus Christ as my Lord and Savior. I wouldn't even be sure what that meant. I also had to balance my intellectual skepticism against any such claim. My meetings with JAC were extremely pleasant. He was about seventy, and would give me interesting books to read that were at least a generation old, including William Temple's *Gospel According to St. John* and Charles Williams's *The Descent of the Dove*. I liked them for their mustiness.

I asked him about sex. He said, as far as the seven deadly sins were concerned, it was bottom of the barrel. Pride was the paramount sin, he added: "It's what separates us from God." *That* resonated with me. I told him about my father, and he took it in stride. I'm sure he had heard it all before. Finally, we got around to Jesus Christ and, there, I confess, I punted. Without touching on Jesus's divinity or Messiahship, I simply stated that I would make Jesus Christ the absolute foundation on which I'd base the rest of my life. It was a studied confession, but JAC seemed satisfied. I was baptized at that year's Easter Vigil by the Advent's then-Rector, Andrew C. Mead, with JAC at my side.

The Reverend John A. Cranston or JAC

***

When I applied to graduate school almost a half-century ago, I wrote that I am an institutionalist. I believed then and now that institutions not only weave a social fabric, they also form an individual's social psychology. For me, Community Music Center of Boston and Church of the Advent make me who I am today. I could not be David Lapin without them. I am at peace with myself because of them, and I know no greater joy than being part of them.

Chapter 30
Music in the Air

Before the turn of the present century, public radio was still music focused. In Boston one could hear classical music in the morning, pop and Broadway in the afternoon, and jazz in the evening. The programming was curated by legendary announcers like Robert J. Lurtsema, Ron Della Chiesa and Eric Jackson. If you didn't know anything about the symphonies of the British composer Arnold Bax, Robert J. was your man. For the singer Margaret Whiting, you'd turn to Della Chiesa, and *Eric in the Evening* could go on for hours exploring pianist Erroll Garner. It was a musical cornucopia and ultimately all too much for public radio's bean counters. Music died a slow death on the radio as the time allotted to it shrank to insignificance. Today consider yourself lucky if you catch Gustav Mahler at three in the morning. Absent that, your best bet for the classics is Johann Strauss Jr.'s *Blue Danube Waltz*. Broadway is kaput, and jazz hobbles gamely in shriveled time.

Robert Della Chiesa happened to live across the street from the Music Center, and it was always a joy for me when he'd drop in to host a recital, usually featuring music therapy students, who were his favorites. Ron was first and foremost a Frank Sinatra devotee, and it was through Ron that I developed my appreciation for the Chairman of the Board and the Great American Songbook.

I was also fortunate to learn a lot about jazz from the Music Center's registrar Tor Snyder. Tor is a guitarist. We talked forever about Chuck Berry, Charlie Byrd, Jimi Hendrix, and the like. We also listened to Coltrane and Miles—all on vinyl, which remains one of my enduring passions. In 1992 I traipsed back on Amtrak from the audio store Stereo Exchange in lower Manhattan with a forty-pound Well Tempered Record Player filled with silicone gel to stabilize the tone arm and the platter. Maybe half of the gel oozed out when the cabbie on the way to Penn Station turned the player on its side in order to fit it into the car trunk. I still play vinyl on that turntable and another former Music Center guitarist, Wayne Potash, inherits it when I buy the farm. Tor gets my Vandersteen speakers.

A comical coda on my record player purchase: I couldn't carry both the turntable and the dust cover back to Boston, so the salesman at Stereo Exchange turned to his stock boy and officiously ordered him to send the dust cover to me via UPS. A few days later, two cartons arrived from New York. The lighter one contained the dust cover. The much heavier package was a mystery. Thinking I might be getting a surprise gift, I opened it only to discover the cinder block on which the dust cover had been perched at the store. To this day, I can't decide if delivering the cinder block was stock boy revenge or just sheer stupidity. I tend to favor the latter.

***

From Joan Rice in 1983 to Mary Carney in 2017, I had the good fortune of reporting to ten board presidents, who also happened to be my friends. Executive directors walk a fine line between cultivating personal relationships with their officers and being held accountable to them. It isn't always easy, but I prefer that structure of authority to the competing model where the chief executive officer is also president and a voting board member.

In the mid-1980s, Cyrus P. Durgin succeeded Lincoln Hansel as treasurer. Known as Peter, his father—also Cyrus Durgin—had been a music critic for *The Boston Globe*. Peter made the case for switching the Music Center to what he called the Harvard model, that is, where the president and CEO's roles are fused. It seemed a bit pretentious to me, and the motion lost decisively. Gracious in defeat, Durgin continued to serve on the board. In my thirty-four years as executive director, I don't think I lost one board member to personal pique or ill will. That had little to do with me, but rather to the Music Center's unifying mission that brings together leaders of diverse backgrounds and politics who work for the good of the students we serve.

Peter's presidents were Mary O. Shannon and Virginia M. Lawrence, also known as Ginger. A Music Center parent, I asked Ginger to help produce my first fundraiser in 1984. We planned a festive celebration of Johann Sebastian Bach's 299th birthday at Harvard's Busch Reisinger Museum, a splendid setting for Baroque music. Planning with Ginger went smoothly, but upon arriving at the Museum on the evening of the event, we discovered that all the paintings and tapestries had been removed from the main hall where we'd be seated. "Security concerns" was the Museum staff's curt explanation. To which Ginger offered an apt rejoinder, "Why on earth did you think we picked the Museum in the first place?"

We got absolutely nowhere, not even scoring a discount, but there was more. The staff told us that at evening's end, we would have to take all our garbage with us! Fortunately, Ginger had brought her station wagon, and around midnight, we begrudgingly loaded the refuse into the rear of the car. At some point, and without much thought, I had retrieved a floral centerpiece from the dais and placed it on top of the station wagon while loading the garbage bags. I then completely forgot about it. Imagine my surprise when, upon arriving in the South End all the way from Cambridge, I discovered the flowers exactly where I had left them. They hadn't moved an inch. And Ginger is not known for slow driving. Ginger was elected board president later that year, and it was she who was largely responsible for stewardship of the Music Center during its move from the Pennock Building to the Cyclorama in 1990.

***

None of my board presidents was a professional musician. But starting with John Kleshinski in 2004, each has felt that his or her job performance would profit from the study of an instrument. John was an incredibly nervous pianist in recitals. His hands would shake violently between phrases. Barbara Roberts is just the opposite—total cool. Out of the blue, she decided to study banjo. She is pretty good and a damn good singer to boot. Following his friend John's preference for piano, Kurt Cerulli has progressed to the stage where he fluently plays Mozart sonatas. And Mary Carney, following Barbara's unusual pick, studies the dulcimer. I don't know what to read into this musical bouquet, except to state the obvious: the guys play it safe when it comes to choice of instruments, while the gals go for *outré* options.

As for Brainiac, early in my Music Center career, I took up the violin. If you are an adult thinking of studying violin, DON'T. I can think of no more unforgiving avocation for a beginner past eight or nine years, and preferably younger. Try cello, instead. I have also sung on many occasions, everything from "Every Time I Feel the Spirit" to a Reader's Digest version of

Don Giovanni (I was the *Commendatore*, not the *Don*.). These vocal entertainments certainly offered me more pleasure than my audience.

Today, I study harpsichord with my teacher Nickolai Sheikov. For some dense reason, I thought the harpsichord touch would be closer to the organ than the piano. As a result of my teenage dalliance with the Hammond organ, I never developed the finger strength that piano requires. I thought the harpsichord would be more aligned with my digital abilities. Wrong, wrong, wrong, because if there's one thing I can count on Nickolai telling me at almost every lesson it's "David, lighten your touch, lighten your touch."

Chapter 31
Water, Water, Every Where

Compared with the tumult of the eighties, work at the Music Center in the nineties was *Calm Sea and Prosperous Voyage*, to borrow the title from Felix Mendelssohn's musical overture. President George H. W. Bush's unfortunate (for him) recession put a brief dent in our finances, but overall we proceeded like a stately ship through untroubled waters. Save for the water itself.

To this day, I have nightmares that the Music Center is being flooded. Water either pours down from the ceiling or up from below. We had left our decrepit 48 Warren Avenue quarters on a Friday morning in March 1990, and were set up in our spic-and-span new home at 34 Warren Avenue four days later. It all seemed too good to be true, and it was. At the end of our first week, bathroom problems occupied my full attention. Water and poop would unpredictably surface from the floor drain in the women's room. It didn't make any sense until a camera probe revealed what had happened. In a cost saving strategy, the building contractor had connected our new plumbing to the building's old system of pipes. The trouble was the pipes weren't for waste. They were part of a French drainage network of perforated conduits that allowed water—but not poop—to seep down below the building foundation.

Our new home was in the ground floor and basement of Boston's historic Cyclorama, which had opened in the 1880s to showcase an exhibition on the Battle of Gettysburg. The original mural is now at the Gettysburg Museum in Pennsylvania. Once Gettysburg was dismantled, the building fell into disuse. By the 1920s it had become a venue for flower wholesalers, and huge concrete tubs were installed to house the flowers overnight. A lot of water must have flowed regularly into the space, and the French pipes were perfect for handling the overflow. Unfortunately, that did nothing for us, except cause me a major headache.

Our architect, Chia-Ming Sze, came up with an ingenious solution. He proposed introducing a gigantic cistern and ejector pump to our plumbing with an entirely new waste line running above the basement floor. The old line would be capped and sealed. The trick would be how to install all of this in a school that was open for business six days a week. We couldn't afford to close for repairs so soon after opening. But we also couldn't function with poop coming up through the floor.

The space next to ours in the Cyclorama had been designated for Boston Ballet's wardrobe shop. The Ballet had not yet moved in, and so with their cooperation, we blasted a hole in our adjoining wall and moved the cistern and all the paraphernalia through their unoccupied space. The cistern was lowered into the floor of a large storage area in our territory that never saw public traffic. The project took about a week to complete, and none of our students was the wiser for it. My plumbing nightmare had ended.

Almost. The ejector pump would periodically malfunction, causing overflows in the cistern *and* the women's room. Our staff was very good natured throughout the whole ordeal, especially my associate director and head of good cheer, Calvin T. Herst, who shared mopping duties with me on an ongoing, as-needed basis.

***

Then there was water from above. Like the old Pennock Building that we had departed, the Cyclorama was the definition of deferred maintenance. Our new space may have been state of the art; but the rest of the building, especially the roof, was in a sorry state of disrepair. Even moderate rain would cause our vestibule to resemble a small waterfall. But nothing could have prepared us for the inundation of June 1998, when nine inches of rain fell on Boston in three hours. It was a Saturday afternoon, which meant we were at the height of our schedule. Out of nowhere, the sky turned black, and rains came with tempestuous force. I could see water rapidly building up on the side of the building until it reached a window and began pouring in. Within ten minutes we were completely flooded. Two of my favorite students, Dan Restuccia and Schumann Robert—yes, you read that right—continued playing as if nothing unusual was happening, but finally even they got the message and fled.

And then it was all over except for the mopping. My closest Music Center friends are Karen and Greg Dimit. They had actually moved to Warren Avenue to be near the Music Center, where Karen, a dramatic soprano, would rehearse. Fortunately, their condo across the street had barely leaked, so both of them rushed over to help me clean up. My main concern was the sprung oak floor in Allen Hall, our concert space. The three of us spent a couple of hours drying the floors, installing fans, and doing our darndest to salvage sodden instruments and the like.

Finally, we escaped to Aquitaine, one of the few nearby watering holes that had survived the inundation. By then, the sun was out and the sky had turned absolutely brilliant. We had just ordered our food when the waiter came over with a bottle of wine. We hadn't ordered it and were a bit perplexed until he pointed to the couple a few tables away from us. It was none other than John Kleshinski and his wife Emily Paul. They figured we had been swabbing the Music Center deck—hence the wine as recompense.

Sunday was just spectacular. Dan Restuccia was leaving Boston Latin for Brown University, and I attended his graduation party in Jamaica Plain that afternoon. It was the first of many occasions for regaling an audience with my Music Center water stories. Not too soon after, the Boston Center for the Arts commissioned a campaign to raise funds for a new roof for the Cyclorama. The project was successfully completed (a rarity then at the BCA), and since then, I'm happy to say, the Music Center's and my water woes are largely behind us.

Except, of course, for the nightmares, which rain on me to this day.

Interlude

We interrupt this memoir to bring you a special message from Brainiac's best friend of fifty plus years, Edward D. Feuerstein.

Brainiac has assigned me the task of describing our annual summer expeditions to Provincetown, which commenced in 1990 and have continued with one exception for twenty-nine "straight" years.

Provincetown is located at the furthest tip of Cape Cod. For generations, it's been one of the East Coast's gayest Meccas. It has also been a haven for artists and writers since the storied Provincetown Players helped launch Eugene O'Neill's career in 1916. Our attraction to "P-town," as it is commonly called, resides in on our living quarters at the Bull Ring Wharf. Originally built as Knowles Wharf in the late 1880s, the Wharf once housed the Casino, a louche entertainment venue and eatery, which was lost to a ferocious 1926 nor'easter that tore through town and leveled much of Commercial Street, the main drag.

Conveniently located near the center of town, the Bull Ring sits on the bay side of Commercial Street, sloping dangerously close to the beach and the bay itself. Our two-bedroom unit, number 10, is on the second floor furthest from the water, although only about a minute's walk from an expansive common deck. The apartment, like all the others, originally sported wide-planked pine floors, painted marine red and splotched with black and white drops. All the walls were glossy beige and the living room boasted a braided rug that housed microorganisms dating back to 1926. There was no air conditioning, no fans, a barely-functioning black and white TV with a wire hanger antenna, and no phone. I used to annoy the hell out of Brainiac by making ultra long and loud business calls in my New Yorker's voice from an outdoor pay phone directly under our living room. "Just live with it," I advised.

The bathroom had decent water pressure and hot water, as long as you got to it before everyone else in the building. The bathroom sink had separate hot and cold faucets, so when you washed your hands, you had to run them continuously left to right and back, or risk being burned. The kitchen was pure 1950s.

***

We loved the Bull Ring in those early years, even when it became ferociously hot under the August sun. Packing for our stay always meant bringing along at least two floor fans, which took precedence in the car trunk over the luggage. All the units contained identical living room furnishings, including a simple Florida day bed in lieu of a sofa and a marine-green wrought iron and glass table complemented by matching chairs with plastic waffle seating surfaces. The bedrooms had surprisingly adequate beds, dressers and closets.

The Florida day bed also allowed us to host a passing parade of visitors for a day or two, which certainly added both to the fun and our popularity among friends from San Diego to Chicago to New York. Over time we also befriended a cast of characters on our annual drive to and from Provincetown. Ever budget conscious, Brainiac would insist on a stop before we hit the Sagamore Bridge, which separates the mainland from the Cape, to buy booze at lower prices than obtainable in P-town. Each year, the same hard-of-hearing lady would ask Brainiac what he wanted, and each year he would yell back PLYMOUTH GIN at least twice. Next door to the package store was a place dearer to my heart—a drive through Burger King. For years, we would make it our business to go into Burger King to order our meals because we looked forward to being greeted by the same bored and slightly brain challenged hostess with the exact same line:

"Welcometoburgerkinghomeof thewhoppermayItakeyourorderplease?"

We always knew our week was off to a good start after that cheery invitation. Unfortunately, last year, Burger King closed and our concern was for the hostess's continued employment. Brainiac has convinced me that another fast food establishment will fill the void and our hostess will return, perhaps with a modified greeting substituting Popeyes or Wendy's as part of her mantra.

***

The Bull Ring has rewarded us over time with an abundance of memorable characters, but none more so than Rosemarie Goodnough and Louise Hagetter or The Girls, for short. They originally occupied a single unit, but for the last decade they've rented a renovated two bedroom, two bath suite opening right onto the deck, with room for a younger companion, Bridget Morton, who now drives them to P-town from New York and back. A better soul in spirit and practice could not be found. When we first met The Girls, they were in their mid-fifties. Now in their eighties, they're a bit slower, but game as ever. They met in a bar in the 1960s and have been a couple ever since.

The Girls: Rosemarie, Bridget and Louise

Rosie cannot cook to save her life; Louise was a superb cook, who used to lavish hot and heavy German food on us during our early P-town years. One summer, Louise prepared Wiener Schnitzel and spaetzle, just the right cuisine for ninety-degree weather. We returned the favor the following year, offering broiled fish and vegetables. Louise moved her fork around the plate, barely concealing her indifference. Finally, as I placed raspberries on the table for dessert, she could hold it in no longer. "Where's the ice cream?" Anticipating a fat free meal, she had brought along her own pint of Häagen Dazs, which we forgot about till her interrogation. After that fiasco, we annually treated each other to dinner out with The Girls paying one year and us the next. Somewhere along the line, we lost track of whose year it was to treat, so now we go Dutch.

Some years back, The Girls introduced Brainiac and me to the joys of Bingo at the local Veterans of Foreign Wars post, where Rosie never failed to take home some winnings. She would share her good fortune with us afterwards by paying for drinks, usually a Sambuca nightcap or two. We always got a kick out of hearing the emcee's cry, "We've got a Bingo" or "It's a Good Bingo," when someone won the card. Somehow we got into the curious habit of notifying each other after nature's call that we've had a good bingo, and all because The Girls introduced us to the pleasures of the game!

***

Today, Unit 10 has morphed into a very chic condo, upgraded with everything from Wi-Fi to high definition television, air conditioning and an expansive glass-tiled shower, which still provides ample hot water. Our annual week in Provincetown is no longer just a vacation, but more like a ritual cleansing and renewal of our psychic energy. Once it enabled us to return to the demands of our separate careers. Now, it recharges our retirement. We look forward to it every summer and, thank God, The Girls are still our treasured partners.

Chapter 32
A Civic Vision

The Clinton years brought unbridled prosperity to Boston and the Music Center. Demographic changes meant more students from affluent families who could pay full tuition. At the same time, we were able to raise more money for scholarships, so the balances among rich, poor, and in-between remained relatively stable. Moreover, for the first time, our work received national prominence as the Lila Wallace-Reader's Digest Fund spearheaded a six-year commitment toward faculty development and tuition assistance. From my perspective, it was the best of all possible times.

I also branched out toward greater personal prominence in the field. The National Guild of Community Schools of the Arts—now the National Guild for Community Arts Education—was run by the wife and husband team of Lolita and Azim Mayadas. Lolita was the charismatic executive director and Azim headed membership. He had a prodigious ability to recall minutiae about any of the Guild's several hundred organizations, and he oversaw applications for membership with the same fine-toothed comb.

By 1990 Azim and Lolita asked me to join the Guild's board of directors and also chair the membership committee. I dutifully accepted and spent my fortieth birthday delivering nominations at the Guild's annual conference, which happened to be in Boston that November. After the report was rendered, I excused myself to attend a birthday lunch at the Ritz Carlton with Ginger Lawrence, who had recently stepped down as the Music Center's board president. I was busy eating when I felt a tap on my shoulder, turned around, and encountered a gorilla trying to hand me a giant bouquet of balloons. I tried walking home, inconspicuous as possible, but that's hard to do when you're holding a dozen oversized balloons briskly blowing in the Boston breeze.

After that interlude, I returned to the conference and Azim and Lolita. Indian by birth, they were a colorful duo, she being the more volatile of the two and he steady as she goes. Azim is an Episcopalian so I had that much in common with him. I was also fascinated by his past career as a concert pianist. Basically, we complemented each other famously and got along fine.

Born before Vladimir Nabokov's novel gave the name its dicey connotation, Lolita was a superb and visionary leader who also occasionally got into fights with a few board members. Guild conferences could end with Lolita in tears arguing with the conference chairs over how successful or not the conference had been. I noted this pattern and thus was not surprised when I began to experience Lolita's ire myself. I knew I was really in trouble when she would address me as if she were a third person in the room. She once actually implored me as other board members fled the scene: "Why are you doing this to Lolita?" For the life of me, I can't recall what I was doing, except perhaps disagreeing with her, which she found eminently disagreeable.

Things between us came to a head in 1997 at the National Guild's sixtieth-anniversary conference and gala concert in Philadelphia. The Guild was always short of staff and relied excessively on local Guild schools to help produce the annual conference. The Settlement Music School was feeling particularly aggrieved in carrying the Philadelphia conference and concert burden on its shoulders. Settlement's executive director Bob Capanna resented Lolita's attempts to change the student orchestra repertoire, which had already been finalized by the conductor Leonard Slatkin. I was then president of the Guild board, and had the responsibility for making concluding comments after the concert at the Academy of Music. I got up and thanked Capanna and Settlement for contributing to the conference's success. I notably left off Lolita's name, and as soon as I returned to my seat, Azim came over to scold me. "How could you do this to Lolita?" I think is what he said. Well, things went downhill from there, and at the next board meeting in New York, I signaled my intention not to run for re-election.

I don't regret that decision, but I did learn that you don't effect much change by resigning one's position. The Guild survived, and Lolita and I made up two years later at the conference in Boulder, Colorado. Azim and Lolita subsequently visited me at the Music Center. Yes, I would handle the fracas differently now, but in my forties, I still allowed pique to get the better of me. Looking back today, I have only fond thoughts of my association with Lolita and Azim Mayadas. They were both incredibly dedicated to the community school movement and the field, and I will always owe them a huge debt of gratitude.

***

Fortunately, I proved less waspish in my other volunteer role. Eric Wodlinger succeeded Ginger Lawrence as president of the Music Center, and became the only person in my tenure as executive director to hold the post for more than four years. A real estate attorney by vocation, Eric had been brought in by Joan Rice to handle the Music Center's Byzantine lease negotiations with the Boston Center for Arts. He also represented the Massachusetts Turnpike Authority, which had a long-run goal of developing the air rights over the Turnpike. By the late 1990s the economics for undertaking such expensive construction seemed promising, and Boston Mayor Thomas M. Menino put together a blue-ribbon panel of citizens to study the topic. The Turnpike Authority had three nominations to the committee, and Eric wanted me to be one of them. I said no twice. The third time I gave in.

I'm not sure why I finally said yes, but it was probably because it had become easier than saying no. Many of my life decisions have been made like that. What I could not have known in 1997 was that I would still be working on air rights development twenty-two years later. And in that time not one Turnpike parcel has been developed! For me, this experience has been an object lesson in democratic dysfunction and an antidote to my graduate school affinity for grassroots community action. I still see the value of participation—why else would I have hung around for almost a quarter century?—but there's also something to be said for leaders taking decisive action.

Eric Wodlinger and Tom Menino were both strong and effective political players. No Music Center president outperformed Eric, and no mayor did a finer job than Tom Menino. In my politician's hall of fame, I would place Menino right next to my childhood hero Nelson Rockefeller. Sad to say, neither Wodlinger nor Menino lived long enough to see the fruits of their labor. Someday those parcels will be developed, and a divide that has separated neighborhoods for generations will be removed. The city will be woven more tightly together, and its residents will have Eric Wodlinger and Tom Menino to thank for that.

Mayor Tom Menino thanking me for my Civic Vision service

***

Through the years I have volunteered for many civic and nonprofit associations. There is delight and contentment in such pursuits, along with the occasional frustrations. If more people got involved in these common causes, I'm certain we'd be less divisive and tribal in our politics. We'd hear and understand opposing points of view, even without agreeing with them. For me, civic engagement is like private prayer. Whatever outcomes either brings forth, they also can be their own reward. For what it's worth, I have no intention of giving up on either.

Chapter 33
Evil

On the morning of September 11, 2001, I got a rare telephone call at work from my brother Jonny. "Call your mother," he commanded. "A plane out of Boston has crashed into the World Trade Center." I heard what he said, but I had difficulty processing it, the same experience I had on hearing that President Kennedy had been shot in 1963. "She'll worry that you were on the plane."

As irrational as his last statement was, I knew my mother well enough to comply with Jonny's order. I called Mom to tell her I was alright, by which time another plane had taken down the second tower. I got off the phone, and had to tell parents in our early childhood classes what had happened. Most like me registered disbelief. Some cried. Almost all of them tried calling loved ones, but the cellular lines were overtaxed, and few calls got through. I canceled all classes and lessons for the day—the first time I had ever done that except for snow—and walked out into the beautiful sun-filled street.

An eerie silence had descended over the South End, and I instinctively looked toward the Prudential and Hancock buildings—Boston's tallest towers— to convince myself they were still there. All of a sudden, the silence was broken by the screaming sounds of Air Force jets flying over the city. In my two decades in Boston, I had never seen a fighter jet enter its airspace.

I walked aimlessly along Tremont Street and bumped into Liane Crawford, a Music Center parent, student and supporter with whom I had once traveled to Chicago on Amtrak. She had left work to go home to her family, but the two of us decided to stop for coffee to talk about what had happened.

I started the conversation by making some incredibly gauche comments about George W. Bush's culpability for letting down our defenses. Liane immediately put me in my place with an "Ah, come on, give the guy a break" riposte, and I knew she was right. This was not a time for partisan divide and the blame game. We needed to show civility and by that afternoon even Boston car drivers seemed respectful of pedestrians, their usual targets.

The following Sunday, Allan B. Warren III, Rector at the Church of the Advent, gave a sermon on the irreducibility of evil. It struck a chord in me then, and it still resonates now. We can psychologize to our heart's content. We can proffer sociological explanations for aberrant behavior. And yet, neither psychology nor sociology can explain away evil. That worm resides in human souls who open themselves to it. It is opposed to all that is good within us, and it is, by our fallen nature, irreducible.

I don't recall how many days we remained closed. Only one of our students lost a family member in the attack, but that was one too many. Ultimately, like everyone, we moved on. But the damage had been done, and America's innocence was lost yet again.

***

Nonprofits are especially hard hit by recessions as earned and contributed income tend to shrink in tandem. The only offset comes in drawing down endowments, and fortunately by 2001 we had built a modest investment portfolio to help us weather the downturn. And unlike the Great Recession seven years in the future, we didn't need to resort to across-the-board salary cuts. Still, it was rough sledding through the winter of 2001-2, but we got through largely unscathed. The same could not be said for several of our sister organizations in the arts. They had to close, and the cultural scene in the Hub of the Universe was poorer for it. Far more would fold in 2009.

My fifteenth anniversary as executive director had been commemorated in 1998 while Richard Dougherty was board president. Dick was a living link to the Music Center's earliest years, as his aunt, grandmother and great grandmother had preceded him on the board. MacDill Air Force Base outside Tampa had been named after his maternal grandfather, an aerial gunner in World War I. Aside from the flood debacle of 1998, Dick's tenure was mostly peaceful and distinguished by an expanded commitment to music therapy. He left his post in 2000, and has recently returned to the board in support of my successor, Lecolion Washington.

Dick was succeeded by Marilyn Morrissey, the first woman to hold the post in a decade. A registered nurse, Marilyn and her husband, Jim Ryan, had three children, all of whom were raised at the Music Center and Boston's public schools. The oldest, Sean Ryan, was a musical standout, and I date the Music Center's growth in curricular and pedagogical quality to our need to rise to the challenges of four extraordinary students of that era: Sean, his best friend Dan Restuccia, our piano chair Will Fickes' son Eric Carty-Fickes, and a truly extraordinary pianist from China, Yangwei Situ. All four were exceptional. Dan especially seemed intent on shadowing me as executive-director-in-training.

In 2005 I traveled to Kunming, China, to visit Yangwei's parents, who I knew from their stay in Boston the prior decade. I was honored to officiate at Yangwei's wedding in 2006. She made a special one-day trip to Boston from Ann Arbor in 2017 just to say goodbye to me as executive director. Around 1993 I thought about heading the Boston Center for Adult Education. Someone made an offhand comment to me at the time: "Won't you miss being around the kids?" The truth is I hadn't given it any thought. But the longer I considered the question, the more I knew I'd be staying right where I belonged. It was the last time I considered leaving the Community Music Center of Boston.

***

National tragedies often bind us closer together. But in ordinary times, institutions like the Music Center serve the same function. They mediate. They help us to respect differences, but they also help us to transcend differences. They don't eliminate class disparities, but they allow individuals from more fortunate circumstances to help those less favored. Some would criticize this role as patronizing. Others go further, arguing that mediating institutions reinforce entrenched structures of oppression. So be it. After thirty-six years at the Music Center, I am prejudiced. We could do a lot worse. And nothing stops us from aspiring to do a lot better. Politically, I'll always stay right in the middle. That's where I believe the most good can be accomplished in the long run, and no one should feel ashamed for striving to achieve just that.

Chapter 34
Travels Domestic and Foreign

Athens, Paris, Florence, Rome, Sydney, Melbourne, Tokyo, Kyoto, Buenos Aires, Caracas, Edinburgh, London, Beijing. Been there, done that, often with my New Haven housemate John Treat, whom I sponged off of in Australia, Japan and Argentina. I think we split the China cost so I could earn Hilton Honors points. But typically, John would provide the room, and I provided the good cheer and maybe a dinner or two.

My first trip as executive director was in 1984 to Detroit, of all places. It was also my first National Guild conference, and we stayed at the futuristic, super cool (not in the good sense) Renaissance Center. Walking the streets downtown was an experience. No one was out and about. I went one evening with my friend Walter Jaffe to the London Chop House, and sat next to Ted Turner. What Ted was doing in the Motor City I do not recall, if I ever knew. I do remember having a spirited sediment called *Marc de Champagne* for the first and only time. Wally and I made it a habit for the next few years to meet at Guild conferences and patronize revolving restaurants, a lost vogue of the nineteen eighties.

***

David E. Lapin

In 1986 Edward Feuerstein and I took a three week trip to the west coast and back. It was my longest Music Center absence, except for a three month sabbatical in 2002. We had agreed to travel exclusively by train. I left from Boston, and Edward departed from Grand Central Station on the *Lake Shore Limited*. We met in Albany, where he joined me in something called a double slumbercoach. It was on an old Heritage car from the Pennsylvania Railroad, I think, and Amtrak phased it out of operation shortly after we experienced its distinctive comforts. The slumbercoach indeed slept two, bunk style, but in its daytime configuration there was room really for no more than three knees. Still, waking up to a glorious sunrise on Lake Erie made it worthwhile.

In Chicago we switched to a luxury Superliner bedroom with bath and shower on Amtrak's now defunct *Pioneer* service to Seattle. Losing this train is an American tragedy because the scenery between Denver and Seattle via Pocatello, Idaho is the most breathtaking I have ever experienced. We traveled for hours without seeing any nasty evidence of humankind. Wildlife and mountain scenery abounded. If I wasn't religious, I'd say it was a religious experience. It certainly felt transcendent.

We arrived in Seattle to be greeted by John Treat, who was then a professor of Japanese at the University of Washington. Expecting to find us looking like survivors from the wreck of the Hesperus, he was stunned to encounter two fully refreshed and relaxed beings, despite our three day journey. Train travel isn't for everybody. But for me, it's kind of like opera and baseball. If you're willing to suspend your sense of time, the effect can be magical. Otherwise, you'll find it excruciating.

John and me in Seattle, 1986

We spent a few days in Seattle and Vancouver, but our main destination was Hollywood, where we would attend the forty-ninth annual "Clan Clave" of the Jeanette MacDonald International Fan Club. Jeanette had come up with the term Clan Clave to describe her fans' gatherings, and she had also anointed Clara Rhodes, an elementary school teacher from Topeka, Kansas, as the Club president. I had joined the Club in 1981, when the Boston Public Library produced a summer tribute to Jeanette. My motives were decidedly mixed, part snarky, part curiosity. I was quickly converted by Clara and the Club members decades' long commitment to Jeanette, a dedication shared by MacDonald's professional colleagues, many of whom attended the Clan Claves as celebrity guests.

All told, I attended six weeklong Clan Claves between 1986 and 1999. Though each ended with a gala banquet, the first was pretty special. As always, Jeanette's husband Gene Raymond presided alongside Clara, although on this occasion he seemed tipsy and cranky. Mary Pickford's widower Buddy

Rogers was on hand to steady Gene. (Buddy, Mary, Jeanette and Gene had all boarded the same steamer for Honolulu after their respective weddings in 1937.) The actor Lew Ayres, who worked with Jeanette on the film *Broadway Serenade* in 1939, also represented old Hollywood. But Edward and I were most excited by the presence of the Golden Girl herself, Beatrice Arthur. Bea didn't have much of any connection to Jeanette, but she also didn't have anything better to do that evening, so she came as the guest of the onetime juvenile actor Robert Arthur (no relation), who basically no one knew.

Robert Arthur also brought Christine Jorgensen, the first American to have had sex reassignment surgery, in 1951. Jorgensen had become a nightclub entertainer shortly thereafter. Apparently, both she and Jeanette were headlining simultaneously in Las Vegas around 1953, and Christine recounted how few people in the industry would have anything to do with her at that time. She was, therefore, all the more grateful when she received an invitation from Jeanette to have tea together. It was a welcome gesture, and Jorgensen came to the banquet to acknowledge Jeanette's kindness. She was, in fact, very moving, though all I could think about at the time was how nicely this matronly lady would fit in at any suburban Kiwanis Club meeting.

***

Later Clan Claves had their merits. The banquet was moved from the Beverly Hilton to the Beverly Wilshire at Gene's suggestion. It was, after all, where the "MacRaymonds" had their wedding reception in 1937. We continued to watch Jeanette films at a dinky civic club, but we also went annually to the Directors Guild of America where we could catch Jeanette in glorious 35 millimeter Technicolor.

Clan Clave 1997 at the Beverly Wilshire, where
Edward won a portrait of Jeanette

By 1999 Jeanette's Clan was getting a little long in the tooth. But there was a huge event to celebrate that summer, and that was the publication by the University of California Press of Edward Baron Turk's prize winning opus, *Hollywood Diva: A Biography of Jeanette MacDonald*. And yes, I had badgered my harried housemate into writing what I felt was a sorely needed reassessment of motion pictures's first musical superstar. The book went on to become one of the Press' best sellers, and I'm still honored twenty years later that Edward dedicated the book "To David E. Lapin, for awakening me to MacDonald" and the "beauty, grace, and gallantry" which the soprano had once embodied for millions of filmgoers worldwide.

***

In my early years at the Music Center, summers were fairly slow. We didn't have air conditioning and few students cared to swelter through lessons in windowless studios. As a result, demands on the staff were pretty relaxed, and I even recall a couple of occasions when Calvin Herst and I would simply leave in the middle of the day for the beach. All that changed in 1990 when we added a daily summer arts program, thanks to air conditioning in the Cyclorama. From then forward, summers became busier than ever. But rest and recharging one's batteries are essential to anyone's long-run job satisfaction, and my summer interludes away from work made possible my annual return to the helm for thirty-four amazing years.

Chapter 35
Panic Attacks

I can recall two panic attacks while traveling overseas. One was at the airport in Beijing. The second extended from Siena to the five towns or *Cinque Terre* that dot Italy's Ligurian coast.

Traveling in Japan and China isn't like traveling in France and Italy. It's easier. There's no need to try and figure out what someone is saying, or what a sign indicates—unless you're among the tiniest minority of Americans who read Mandarin, Cantonese, or Japanese. When I use the subways in Tokyo, Kyoto and Beijing, I count the number of stops the train needs to make before arriving at my destination. There are some lines with Roman lettering, but you can't depend on it. I remember once getting off at a subway stop in Beijing, only to discover that I was still about a mile from my destination. The solution is to hail a taxi, and bring with you a card indicating where you want to go. Maybe Uber has usurped that highly efficient method by now.

When I traveled in 2005 to the city of Kunming, which is north of Vietnam, I managed to secure a round trip ticket at the airport in Beijing with no problem, though Yangwei's family had already set up my reservation and paid for it. There was a last minute change at the gate, which briefly unsettled me. The gate I had been assigned was boarding a flight for Shanghai, not Kunming. But saying "Kunming?" And hearing something like "No, Shanghai," prevented me from boarding the wrong plane. I can't remember how I figured out which gate I needed to walk to, but I probably just followed the small herd who had been similarly displaced.

Leaving Beijing for the States was a different matter. I had gotten to the airport early and by myself. John Treat had left the previous day. No problem, I thought, until I tried to ascertain which gate United Airlines would use for my flight to Chicago. Nothing appeared that I could discern on the departure screens. And no one, contrary to what you read in Fodor, spoke English. I must have spent the better part of an hour trying to figure out where I was supposed to go. Finally, with visions of living at the Beijing airport as my ultimate destiny, I backed into a group that may have passed for Americans. I joined them, but I swear, I never saw any sign or indication that this was the line for Chicago until I showed my ticket to the attendant who checked me in for boarding.

***

My Beijing snafu was a teeny blip compared to what happened in Italy in 1994. The plan was for me to meet an American friend in Milan. I would take TWA's nonstop flight from Boston and he would take a train from Paris. We would meet at the Milan train station. The first hurdle was a strike by the transportation workers who moved passengers from Malpensa Airport into Milan. I learned the word for strike in Italian, *sciopero*, though some insisted that *strike*—streekay—was also acceptable (not in a million years).

The *sciopero* was over in about an hour. Italian strikes are frequent but I learned they're often brief. I got in a taxi and proceeded into the city, suspecting that my cabbie was taking the longest possible route. He insisted it was long, but it was also the shortest, time wise. Who was I to contest such logic?

I finally got to my hotel, and I knew I needed to grab another cab almost instantly and go to the train station. I arrived at the station only to discover that the train workers were also on strike. No problem, everyone in the station just seemed to doze off, except me. I had promised my friend we would meet at the station no matter what, but I hadn't counted on another *sciopero* interfering with the train's arrival. Not knowing how long this latest strike would last, I decided to return to the hotel.

"You said you would meet me at the train station no matter what," I was admonished about an hour later. "I know, but I didn't count on a strike. There was no way of knowing how long you'd be delayed." There was truth to both sides, but the fun had just begun.

We left Milan a couple of days later and headed for a charming *agriturismo* inn called *Monte Pù*. It would serve as our base for exploring the nearby Ligurian coast south of Genoa. *Monte Pù* could have been the setting for a movie version of Thomas Mann's *The Magic Mountain*. We left on our first full day for Siena in a manual shift rental which I couldn't drive. (Calvin Herst had once tried to teach me how to operate a stick shift and clutch, but the attempt proved wildly unsuccessful.) We parked somewhere near the main piazza, and began to explore the town, especially the mosaics in the floor of the Cathedral. We weren't mindful of the time, until dusk was about to settle. We tried to retrace our way to the car to no avail. We made the classic error of asking native passersby, who were more inclined to give us misleading directions than no response at all.

The sign on the left says "Mangia," in Siena, Italy

Somehow, we stumbled onto the car and began our God forsaken journey back to *Monte Pù*. Traveling close to the coast, we took the only routes we encountered, all with the warning *Strada Disastrosa* or disastrous road. "How bad could it be?" I ventured. BEYOND BAD would have been the appropriate response. In fact, we were clinging to dear life next to precipices that no Italian motorist would ever think of approaching. Boulders also blocked our way, and I could not bring myself to look out the right side of the car, for fear of seeing absolutely nothing below. Residents of the *Cinque Terre* take trains and funiculars to get around, leaving their disastrous roads to unsuspecting tourists.

After an hour or two of this torture (and with the setting sun providing less and less light), we caught up with a second car ahead of us that had made the same trip. Fortunately, it looked like our joint nightmare was over as a bona fide highway suddenly appeared before our eyes. But first, the car ahead of us stopped, and a woman got out on her hands and knees and kissed the ground. Then she came over to corroborate what she and her husband had just been through—the worst driving nightmare of their lives. They were Israeli tourists and, like us, they had pooh-poohed the cautionary note of *Strada Disastrosa*.

About forty minutes later, we entered our sanctuary at *Monte Pù*, wiser to the ways of driving, Italian style. I have been told that the roads along the Amalfi coast on Italy's eastern flank are equally treacherous. With all due respect to those who have been there, I would have to disagree. I have done many dumb things in my life. But nothing rivals the sheer terror of boldly going where no man with half his marbles has foolishly gone before.

Chapter 36
"Follow the Fumes"

By 2002, I had worked at the Music Center for twenty-one years, and I needed a longer break than a summer vacation afforded. I also felt that the school would profit by being on its own for a while. For the first time, I began thinking about succession planning and the Community Music Center of Boston in a post-Lapin era.

I negotiated a paid sabbatical with Marilyn Morrissey. I would be gone from June through August. Those were the sole agreed-upon terms, which I considered generous, and my thoughts turned to what I would do over three months.

***

Once again, John Treat came to the rescue. We had shared some time together in Japan a couple of years before. This time, he was planning an extended stay in Australia; would I be interested in joining him and his boyfriend Douglas Lind? They had secured an apartment in the Potts Point neighborhood of Sydney, and photos of their posh quarters did nothing to quash my enthusiasm for joining them.

I took the longish flight from Boston to Los Angeles and had a brief wait at the airport before boarding the next plane for Sydney. At the gate I recall thinking how hot the Australians looked. I was definitely going to enjoy this trip until I noticed the time it takes to get there. Sixteen hours seemed longer than any plane was meant to stay in the air. I gulped once or twice, completed another survey of my fellow passengers' pulchritude, and boarded the 747 for Down Under.

My anxiety was unwarranted. Time passed uneventfully, which is more than I can say for the Aussie customs process awaiting me. Someone must have determined that I looked like a subversive because the agent singled me out for special attention, and required me to unpack all my luggage. I had learned years before in Chartres, France, never to challenge a bureaucrat in a foreign country, and so I meekly complied. Out came all the underwear, pants, shirts, swim gear, drugs (the legal kind)—everything one needs for a month's stay.

Satisfied that he had done enough to make me uncomfortable, the agent gave me the green light to leave his bailiwick, and I met John, who had been waiting for me all the while. I had shoved my belongings back in my bags, and thought the worst was over. John got into a tiff with the immigrant cabbie who hadn't heard of Potts Point, but we made it to our destination safe and sound.

Doug was awaiting our arrival, and had prepared wine and cheese to welcome me. I walked out onto the apartment porch and took in the expansive view of the Sydney Harbor Bridge, the Opera House, and downtown. It was a bright, sunny and crisp late afternoon, and a mild winter was about to descend on the Southern Hemisphere. All was right with the world. I finished my drink and went to my own bedroom to unpack. It only took a few moments to suspect to my horror that all my toiletries and medications had been left behind at the airport. We scoured the apartment to no avail—thank you Australian customs man—but I was forced to concede that Brainiac had indeed failed to repack his only important carry-ons.

The next day John accompanied me to Darlinghurst Medical Clinic—just what everyone wants to do when visiting a foreign country for the first time. I learned from the posters in the waiting area that Australians take sun exposure very seriously since their skin cancer rate is quite high, especially for those of European extraction. A modest amount of time elapsed before I got to see Dr. Francis Donoghoe, who listened sympathetically to my story. He had to trust that I was telling the truth, of course, though it wasn't like I was asking for narcotics. I was on statins for borderline high cholesterol and tricyclics to help me sleep. He agreed to write the "scripts" as they call them, but the next hurdle was figuring out what the drugs were called in Australia. After a few minutes' research, he proclaimed "Eureka," wrote the scripts, and I left for the nearest drugstore. I bought my pills, along with a toiletry bag that John claimed was too small for someone my age. He said a bigger one is required the older one gets—more years, more pills and more cosmetics. Well, just to disprove his thesis, I carry that bag around with me to this day though, truth to tell, I usually need to supplement it with a newer Dopp kit.

***

Whenever I'm outside Boston, I always try to find a spiritual substitute for the Church of the Advent. It's never an easy search because the Advent is a high Episcopal, Anglo-Catholic parish. Inspired by the Oxford Movement of the nineteenth century, Anglo-Catholic churches are Eucharist-focused and typically employ ornate liturgies, fancy vestments and smelly incense—things that regular churchgoers find either abhorrent or allergy-inducing.

Even in the Anglican Communion, Anglo-Catholicism is a niche product. And so, when I visit foreign lands, I do research beforehand, which is precisely how I discovered The Parish of St. James, King Street, Sydney. By Advent standards it was high-church lite. No incense. But the liturgy was reasonably orthodox, and on my first Sunday, I offered up a prayer of thanksgiving for Dr. Donoghoe and my new pills.

With the Mass ended, I figured I'd make some new friends at coffee hour. I've never been to an Episcopal or Anglican church that hasn't offered some refreshments post-service, but I didn't see any obvious venue at St. James. I walked down the nave toward the entrance and was greeted as is customary by one of the priests. "Lovely service, Father. Is there a reception?" With a flamboyant wave of his arm, he responded, "Just follow the fumes!" And with that, I proceeded toward the Columbarium, where St. James' departed are interred. This would be a first, I thought, sherry among the departed.

Fortunately, the Columbarium opened onto a garden, where most of the parishioners had already assembled. I, being the new boy in town, found myself surrounded by curious congregants. Chief among these was Graeme Bailey, the Churchwarden, who could not have been more friendly and welcoming. He made me feel right at home, as did members of the Most Venerable Order of the Hospital of St. John of Jerusalem, who were having a special ceremony that afternoon. It was all very gay and friendly—lack of incense, notwithstanding.

With Doug Lind on top of the Sydney Harbor Bridge

Chapter 37
A Retirement Dress Rehearsal

I returned to St. James several times during my stay in Australia, but John had already made plans for us to visit Port Douglas and the Great Barrier Reef. So we left Sydney after a week for my next absurdist adventure. Now, you will have to suspend disbelief for the next few paragraphs because the truth is I hadn't a clue what the Great Barrier Reef is. I thought maybe it was something you looked at like the Statue of Liberty from the Staten Island Ferry.

I don't even think I knew what lay ahead of me once we boarded a catamaran in Port Douglas—though the free dose of Belladonna tipped me off that something unsteady was about to happen. I had taken Belladonna in milk for years after my bout with St. Vitus' Dance, a sure way to fall asleep as a narcotized teenager.

The Belladonna didn't work for most of my fellow travelers, especially a large Japanese contingent who were planning a scuba dive. After about an hour of increasingly rough waves, they all threw up together in the most polite and communal way. John and I just turned green.

Finally, I discovered where and what the Reef is and what I needed to do to see it. John had guessed correctly that if he had told me ahead of time, I wouldn't have dreamt of accompanying him. I was to don a wetsuit, goggles and snorkeling gear, and get thrown overboard. It was all very simple, and the crew assured me that they had never lost a soul because they carefully counted how many were tossed overboard and how many returned. This procedure had been put into place after someone actually was left behind and never recovered.

I had never really snorkeled before and I had the hardest time forming a seal between my mouth and the mouthpiece. A fine young fellow named Garth or Gareth or Graeme was assisting me to no avail until he advised "Think Mick Jagger." It instantly did the trick, and I jumped into the Pacific for my first dive. Unfortunately, the ocean was pretty muddy, and I only dimly saw the legendary reefs. "No problem," said Garth/Gareth/Graeme. "We'll have two more chances."

Taking off a wetsuit is infinitely more challenging than getting it on when it's dry. But lunch was about to be served and I needed to towel down and rest up for dive number two. A lavish spread consisting mostly of crustaceans had been prepared by our mates. John and I must have had the same thought simultaneously, because neither of us ate much—not wanting to see shrimp a second time on the return voyage.

I decided to pass on dive number two—I couldn't conceive of getting in and out of the wetsuit three times—but the last one did the trick. I went down and saw incredibly colorful and prolific formations. It saddens me to think that most of these are lost today to global warming. I consider myself doubly fortunate to have seen them at all.

The catamaran journey back was even worse than getting there. John turned green, then white, then grey—as did I, I'm sure—but our decision to refrain from a hearty lunch had paid off. I can't say the same for our intrepid Japanese colleagues.

***

My Australian adventure had one more near accident when, on our return to Sydney, a cab driver started pulling away from the curb with the heel of my sneaker caught under the taxi's right rear tire. Apparently, he never saw me getting in the cab, such was his attention to detail. I yelled STOP just in the nick of time, otherwise my foot would have been crushed. John, Doug and I rode the rest of our trip in stone silence, appalled at how close I had come to an emergency return visit to Dr. Donoghoe.

After that incident, John and Doug left for Tasmania, while I was intent on visiting Melbourne. I had a friend there named Fay LaGalle, whom I had met at various Clan Claves. She and her husband Keith were very gracious and took me to the countryside to visit the local wineries and vineyards. She had a shed set up in her backyard as a kind of shrine to Jeanette MacDonald, and I could tell that Keith—good sport that he was—still felt slightly uncomfortable about his wife's and my shared passion.

I was also planning to hook up with a hottie I had met earlier in Sydney, who was touring in Melbourne with the Sydney Dance Company. I attended his performance, but as was so typical of me in this chaste decade, I passed on meeting him afterwards. Instead, I went to bed early by myself. I had a long rail journey ahead of me in the morning from Melbourne back to Sydney. I had sprung for business class, which was a waste of money, but I looked forward as usual to a relaxing train trip.

The next day, I boarded about thirty minutes early. Soon thereafter, two passengers took the seats across the aisle from me: a sweet ten-year old girl and her father, who turned out to be a mortician. He was pleasant enough and wanted to know whether undertakers are held in higher esteem in America than in Australia. I didn't really know how to respond to his query, but my Brainiac powers kicked in as I asserted that undertakers in the States often run for elective office, so they are indeed quite popular—or very unpopular, but I didn't say that. He seemed very pleased with my response, and I tried passing the next ten hours focusing more on the scenery than my newfound friends.

On my return to Boston, I discovered eBay, where I bid on lots of old vinyl records and open reel tapes, too successfully in retrospect. eBay kept me busy for the last two months of my sabbatical. But it also taught me that real retirement would require more planning than I had given to this dress rehearsal. It was a good lesson to learn, and I find myself today far more occupied than I ever would have imagined back in 2002.

Chapter 38
The Back

A Sword of Damocles always hangs over my vacation plans and trips abroad, and that is the prospect of hideous, disfiguring back spasms. I was in ninth grade when I bent over one morning in the kitchen to tie my sneakers. A sharp pain went down my right side, and I could barely stand up. I didn't return to school for a week, as the pain persisted until forced bed rest finally kicked the demon into submission.

Since then back pain has been my closest companion, more so than music, politics, religion or sex. It hides for a time and then returns with Medusa-like fury. All I can do when it appears is submit to its will. I never know how long it will last, days, weeks or even months. It has its own life, and I am largely powerless before it. I sometimes think that I stop being myself when it takes hold of me; I become another me—helpless, crippled, and clueless as to how to recover my own nature. My only salvation lies in knowing that it will eventually pass, and I will become my true self once more.

***

Graduate School requires hours of sitting, reading and writing, and many of my colleagues at the time complained of chronic back disorders. In my twenties, the most frequent problem was sciatica, or pain down the side of my right leg. It was more of a nuisance than disabling. By the time I reached my thirties, the real fun began. Perhaps the stress of work compounded the severity of the attacks—though I am loathe to assign any cause to my back and its discontents—and by 1985, days would go by where I had to work lying on my back. I actually interviewed and hired Calvin Herst in Elsbeth Meuth's presence while lying on the floor of my Bay Village living room.

In early 1986 I attended a performance of Handel's very long oratorio *Samson* with Jon Vickers at the Met. I wouldn't have missed it for anything, but I knew I was already in trouble on the train ride down to New York. The pain just got worse as Vickers agonized over his blinded state. By *Samson's* end, I could barely stand up. I must have retreated to Edward Feuerstein's apartment for the night because I can't imagine having taken the train back until the following day.

I returned to Boston in excruciating anguish. Days passed with no relief in sight. I went to see an orthopedic surgeon who recommended Naproxen. Nothing I had tried in the past seemed to work. Finally, I sought counsel from my friends at Boston Ballet who recommended chiropractic—one therapy I still hadn't tried.

They referred me to a doctor in Brookline, which wasn't especially convenient in my bent state. But I took the trolley out to see him, where I was subjected to X-rays and indoctrination on chiropractic. I had to sit through a half-hour video on vertebral subluxation degeneration, and was sent home without relief. That was a Friday afternoon and I'd suffer through the weekend before my scheduled treatment on Monday morning. By that point, I was desperate, and agreed to the terms he laid out.

I returned on Monday and he made one adjustment to my right side. And just like that, the pain was gone. I couldn't believe it—nor could he, I suspect. I had put up with all the mumbo jumbo three days earlier, and here I was cured and able to walk reasonably upright. Who wouldn't be a convert to the one true religion under such circumstances?

I returned twice a week for the next three months. He even recommended a chiropractor for me to see after my train trip that June to Seattle. I was able to resume physical exercise without difficulty and was probably never in better shape in my life. And then, it happened again.

By 1988 I had switched allegiances to a chiropractor closer to my home. I had obtained good results with him before, but this time his chiropractic touch failed to do its charms. I had also taken up swimming as therapy, and that offered some relief (and a sleeker body), but neither swimming nor chiropractic were able to get my condition completely under control.

I also began seeing Stephen Pearson, my general practitioner, and proposed that my inability to relax my back muscles may be related to Stanley's sexual assaults. This was in fact the first time I had ever discussed this topic with anyone, and it set off a round of therapeutic sessions that addressed that issue, while doing precious little for the back.

Once again, the demon left as inexplicably as it had arrived. I was able to take an extended car trip to New Hampshire in 1989 to see a concert by the saxophonist Kenneth Radnofsky, who would succeed Calvin as the Music Center's associate director in 1997. A longtime trustee, Rowland Sturges, and his wife Hedy agreed to drive me while I laid down on the rear seat of their sedan for most of the trip. At one point, Rowland turned around and asked me in his inimitable manner if I wanted "some hooch." I probably would have enjoyed a swig or two, but for some reason, I respectfully declined.

Radnofsky's concert was a big hit and I was clearly on the mend—again. There was a pattern to discern by then. Major incidents were about twelve to eighteen months apart. And they were most likely to occur in the spring, just as I was gearing up for the Music Center's annual fundraiser.

***

The worst episode happened sometime in the mid-nineties. I woke up one morning, got out of bed, and immediately dropped to the floor in writhing agony. My face was covered in sweat from a fever that instantly consumed my body. Trying to get up was pointless. I must have been on the floor for an hour, but who could tell and what difference did it make? Finally, I summoned all my strength at an attempt to scale the bed, and I succeeded.

As soon as practicable, I returned to yet a third chiropracter, who did gentle adjusting supplemented by electrical muscle stimulation. Not only did the latter make my skin crawl. I began to feel pain radiating everywhere from my neck to my heels. That set off a new alarm, and I returned to Stephen Pearson, who immediately referred me to a rheumatologist.

Fibromyalgia was all the vogue back then, and I was thus diagnosed. I went on Doxepin for the next quarter century, the idea being that it would facilitate soft tissue repair through deeper sleep. I guess it worked somewhat, as the symptoms of fibromyalgia ebbed over time. But the Big Kahuna remains with me to this day.

My last major relapse was June 2017, just in time for the first of my two retirement events, so I am overdue. Or just maybe, the demon is done with me now that I've retired. I wouldn't put any money on that possibility, but stranger things have happened. For now, I'll play the waiting game, and that's just fine and dandy, considering the alternative.

Chapter 39
"Gate of Heaven"

Leaving my back problems to fate, faith and watchful waiting, I concentrated my energies on adding new dimensions to my life at the Advent. If these weren't cures for my physical maladies, they did afford me multiple pleasures both spiritual and social (the two are mutually supportive), including making many new friends who enrich my life to this day.

Nancy Nickolds was a middle school principal. She was a rigorous disciplinarian and she brought this virtue to her role as the Advent's warden of acolytes, the person responsible for populating the cast in the drama of the Mass. A crucifer is needed to carry the crucifix. Torchbearers carry, you guessed it, torches. Acolytes assist at the Gospel procession and the liturgy of the Eucharist, and a thurifer is in charge of coals and incense. A lay person assists the priest and deacon as subdeacon, while a master of ceremonies oversees the entire production. It's complicated ritual, and even after a decade at the Advent, I was in awe of the congregants who felt sufficiently competent to discharge these roles on a weekly basis.

***

In 1996 Nancy asked me to volunteer for the Acolyte Guild. I was terrified at the prospect, and I came up with numerous rationalizations for why I would be awful, counting on my back to get me excused. But saying no to a school principal isn't really possible, and I ultimately submitted to Nancy's higher power.

The night before my first "performance," I simply could not sleep. I was scheduled to be a lowly torchbearer, but perfectionism got the better of me, and I was sure I'd make a total fool of myself. The following day, everything went smoothly, though there would be subsequent mishaps, like the time we processed around the church, returned to the altar, and I walked "offstage" by myself, since no one had told me to return to the communion rail along with the other torchbearers. But I had seen gaffes before, and wasn't overly concerned with this particular faux pas.

Tending to the coals as thurifer was another matter. I never had much desire to be the chef at barbecues, and lighting coals for incense is nerve wracking. You have to light the coals with a Bunsen burner. You have to place the ignited coals into a mini-pot, which in turn gets dropped into the base of the thurible. You have to learn to swing the thurible just so, and on high holy days, you need to negotiate three-hundred sixty degree revolutions of the thurible while walking down the church's main aisle and transept. And you have to carry a boat with incense, since the priest may lay on more incense once you arrive at the altar.

One morning, I prepared the coals and got into position to lead the offertory procession, as is the custom. We arrived at the altar footpace, genuflected, and I walked toward the priests to have incense laid. I raised the top of the thurible and, lo and behold, no coals! They had disappeared as in a magic trick, only there was nothing magical about how I felt at that moment. After a stunned second or two, I determined that the pot containing the coals had gotten stuck inside the top half of the thurible. A gentle jingle of the chains caused the pot to dislodge and incense was laid on as if nothing had happened. But my days as thurifer had just sung their swan song. I now cede this responsibility to old pros like Richard Corrieri and Ciaran Della Fera or my younger colleagues Dustin Henderson and Melanie McNaughton—all calmer souls than Brainiac.

My days as thurifer are over.

***

My experience at the Music Center lent credibility to my reputation for fundraising and around 2005 Father Warren asked me to chair the Advent's stewardship campaign. Running a church canvass isn't much different from raising money for secular pursuits. But it does add a spiritual dimension, since giving lies at the core of Christian life. You can't be a stingy Yankee *and* a good Christian, despite many attempts at such.

The Vestry, or governing board of the Church, sets a high bar by recommending a tithe or ten percent of one's income. A few devout souls actually give at that level. I try to give ten percent in toto to all my charities. Giving is essential to being a Christian because it battles against hardness of heart.

The real financial test for the congregation came in 2008, when masonry dislodged in the chancel—fortunately, not during a service—and fell next to the bishop's throne below. Years of deferred maintenance could no longer be ignored, and we had to commit to raising over two-million dollars to repair the steeple, the stained glass, and—above all—the roof. We had done our due diligence in setting a feasible goal, but that was before the Great Recession hit. I had joined the Campaign committee, and just around the time that the market reached rock bottom, Father Warren asked me if I could take over as chair. Well, the good thing about starting at the bottom is knowing there's no place to go but up, and the Campaign for the Advent proceeded toward its successful conclusion with far fewer dropouts than anyone would anticipate even in normal times. Adventers are a hearty and devoted lot, and never more so than when the church needs us. Today, the Advent shines luminously on Beacon Hill's skyline, a potent reminder to all that "this is none other than the house of God, and this is the gate of heaven."

***

The Advent faces east toward Jerusalem and, I believe, toward those departed souls who we knew in life. My Father Confessor John Cranston is one of them. Frederic Clanagan, who I accompanied in 1998 for a pilgrimage to holy sites in Scotland and England, is another. Ann Evans, my longtime Fenway Park companion, is another. Each spring I memorialize them with flowers for Holy Week. The one person I miss the most is

Vance Hosford. A fellow acolyte, Vance was so devoted to the Advent that he drove two hours each Sunday from his home in Vermont to worship with us. Vance was also the Advent's principal architect-in-residence. It was Vance who oversaw the physical restoration of the Advent a decade ago.

Vance's visual aesthetic tended toward the conservative, or "the authentic," as he would describe it. The same applied to his love of music, and we once gave him no end of grief for skipping out on Good Friday for a mediocre performance of *Tosca*. He was also an accomplished organist and actually housed two organs in his Vermont home, which he himself had designed and built. Vance may not have been a Renaissance man, but he came darn close in my estimation. He died too soon of pancreatic cancer, and his fellow acolytes mourn his passing to this day.

The good news is that when we face Jerusalem on Sunday mornings, we're greeting Vance and reminding him that the Church of the Advent stands solid today because of his extraordinary works on her behalf. Can there be a finer memorial than that?

Chapter 40
Storm Signals

The one time Edward Feuerstein and I did not summer in Provincetown was 2006, when the Bull Ring closed for emergency renovations. We had always wanted to visit Santa Fe, and so we decided to journey to New Mexico on Amtrak's *Southwest Chief*. The train trip was about the only thing that seemed to go right that summer. I look back now and see August to November 2006 as the most disturbing months of my adult life.

Edward and I made a decision in 2004 not to purchase unit 10 when the complex converted to condominiums. The asking price was exorbitant and the condition of the property, both inside and out, had so deteriorated that we knew it would take tens of thousands, if not more, just to bring it up to code. I was especially concerned about the lack of a modern fire alarm system and a secondary egress. It turned out that my Cassandra powers—shared by The Girls—were quite prescient. In fall 2005, we were notified that the Bull Ring would be closed indefinitely for extensive repairs to the foundation, which was basically sinking into the bay. The cost ultimately totaled several million dollars, and a few condo owners declared bankruptcy as a result.

Avoiding that quagmire should have augured for good fortune going forward, but just the opposite was true. We had to fly into Chicago to depart on the *Southwest Chief*, and I arranged a short detour to Champaign to check in with Frieda, still living happily by herself in her ninetieth year. A few falls aside, Mom was in remarkably good shape with almost all her marbles intact. She was still capable of keeping her apartment in impeccable order, and though she no longer balanced the checkbook, she had no problem writing checks for ten dollars to every charity that sent her an appeal. Still, I was growing concerned over the frequency of her falls, and leased a Life Alert system to assist her with any future incidents.

Edward and I had a nice stay. She had always treated him as a third son, and his accompanying me was hardly a surprise. After two days, we kissed her goodbye, took our leave, and returned to Chicago. It was the last time either of us would see her.

***

Detraining in Albuquerque meant renting a car for the several hours' trip to Santa Fe. I wasn't sure why at the time, but the process of getting from the train station to the car rental and then driving to Santa Fe in the late afternoon caused me a lot of angst and irritation. I was short with Edward—nothing surprising, there—and I was unduly nervous driving. Something seemed out of whack, but it wasn't dramatic enough for me to give it much thought.

We got to Santa Fe in one piece, and checked into a Hampton Inn on the side of town away from the open amphitheater opera house, which we planned on visiting. Even the short drive to the theater got me upset, but the performance that evening more than compensated. Thomas Adès' *The Tempest* was being given its first American performances. Right before curtain time, a storm had come through. It could not have been better timed, as the opera opens with a storm that casts shipwrecked passengers on Prospero and Caliban's isle. The stage was flooded with water, and the survivors literally came up through the water at their first appearance. It was truly a *coup de théâtre* and unforgettable. The music and drama were first rate, and Edward and I both felt we were witnesses to the present century's first operatic hit.

The next night we returned to see Joyce DiDonato in Jules Massenet's operatic riff on the Cinderella tale, *Cendrillon*. It was magical but seemed pallid after *The Tempest*. (Twelve years later, I would see it again with DiDonato at the Met, and its special charms were more persuasive on that occasion.) When we weren't at the opera, we were sampling Santa Fe cuisine and nightlife. Edward even bought a painting by a young Lakota artist, who subsequently went to Federal prison on a drug conviction. I had developed a mild cough and was feeling out of sorts, so it wasn't with unalloyed sadness that our trip came to a close. I planed back to Boston, and Edward returned to New York, both of us looking forward to returning to P-town in 2007.

***

I wasn't home more than three days when I got a call from Champaign informing me that Mom had fallen again. She had been watching a movie with some of her friends, and upon getting up, fell straight to the floor and suffered a mild shoulder fracture. This was the first time she had ever broken a bone. My brother Jonny had talked to her by phone in the hospital, and she was alert and in good spirits. Nothing seemed out of the ordinary.

A few hours passed and I got a second call from a nurse indicating that Frieda was semi-conscious. For a few seconds, I assumed that the condition was a delayed effect of the fall, and the nurse seemed to confirm that, until I discovered that Mom had suffered a second fall, in the hospital, tumbling upside down and hitting her head on the floor. Someone had forgotten to raise the rails on her bed, and in trying to get to the bathroom, she had sustained an acute subdural hematoma. I wasn't sure whether I was more shocked about the fall or the hospital's negligence. I guess it didn't matter, because three hours later, she was dead.

Mom and me in Champaign, Illinois, 2005

The hospital was required to conduct an inquest, but nothing came of it. Small towns learn to protect their own, especially their only major hospital. I immediately had to return to Champaign, clean out the apartment and begin the arduous process of handling Mom's estate. Edward's presence was never more needed—Jonny's presence would have been burdensome, given his own physical condition—and he planed back to Champaign to offer his assistance and moral support. We somehow got everything shipped or discarded in forty-eight hours. Utterly exhausted to a degree I had never previously experienced, I left Champaign for the last time, mourning Frieda's unnecessary death and contemplating a lawsuit to hold the hospital accountable.

***

By late August, I could no longer ignore my physical decline. The innocuous cough that began in Santa Fe was getting worse. I found even the short walk to the Music Center a challenge. A two-hour appointment with an obnoxious and overly talkative visitor at work utterly destroyed me. By late September, when the Music Center's annual meeting of the corporation occurred, I was a wreck. Part of the problem surely stemmed from the loss of my mother. But an ill-fated dinner with my Advent friend C. Thomas Brown confirmed my worst suspicions. I had become so physically weak that I couldn't get my knife through a pork chop. With that, I returned home, went to bed, and began contemplating my own mortality. I was in dire straits, and nothing seemed more rational at the time than giving thought for the first time to putting my own house and affairs in order.

Chapter 41
Tragedy

Stephen Pearson's tenure as my physician ended around 2004. Like Steve, his successor had what used to be called excellent bedside manners, but whereas Pearson was exceedingly proactive, the new M.D. veered toward laissez faire. In early September 2006, I was told I had viral pneumonia, and was sent home with a prescription for rest and Albuterol. I can't recall any further instructions.

As my condition worsened, I would call the doctor's office, but gatekeepers prevented me from getting through. I became sufficiently concerned to get in touch with Greg Dimit, my executor, who immediately called his wife, Karen, in New York. She came up to help me, as did my former board president Marilyn Morrissey, whose RN skills proved especially helpful. One blood pressure reading was all Marilyn needed to get on the phone, and the doctor took *her* call, if not mine. Marilyn uttered an arcane medical phrase, and that finally got some attention. A half-hour later, I was at Mount Auburn Hospital in Cambridge, where I would spend the next eight days.

John Kleshinski had succeeded Marilyn as Music Center president in 2004. Cognizant of my status, he arranged for me to take a medical leave and asked Will Fickes, who had been promoted to associate director in 2002, to step in as acting director. Meanwhile, unsure of how my situation would play out, I asked Benjamin King, then one of the Advent's curates, to consider at least the possibility that I might not pull through. Ben looked stunned, but agreed to help oversee my funeral, if one should be needed. Perhaps I had played a melodramatic hand, but I was trying to anticipate every outcome, and death didn't seem far fetched at that moment.

Multiple tests were conducted without positive results, though a bronchoscopy produced violent chills and fever. The only discovery I made was that I have a dead mass on the lower lobe of one of my lungs, but nobody could determine if this was caused by my current pneumonia or an earlier episode from my childhood days in Puerto Rico. I was getting nowhere and then a resident appeared who made me laugh. "You are sick because you are depressed," he informed me, "due to your mother's recent death." I told him that my symptoms appeared prior to her demise, so how could her passing be responsible for my state? Without being disingenuous in the slightest, he said "sometimes it works that way." I felt like I was inhabiting the *Twilight Zone*.

Slowly, depression or not, the intravenous feed began to restore my strength. On the eighth day of my hospital stay, the ever helpful Dimits arrived in their Subaru Forester to take me home. I was still weak (my weight had descended to 133 pounds), but there had been enough improvement for me to depart Mount Auburn with some optimism. A brigade of board members took turns delivering soup to me over the next two weeks, and by the third week in November, I was eager to return to work.

Will had performed competently in my absence, as did Claudia Haydon, our development director, who hadn't let one ball drop since my summer decline. And John Kleshinski had done an absolutely bang up job keeping everyone's spirits afloat. The staff and faculty were primed for my return. And then, just as I resumed my labors, tragedy struck the Music Center.

***

When Marilyn and I talked to John about becoming president, we were mindful of his past work at Merck-Medco and the successful career that allowed him to retire in his early fifties. Since then, the Music Center had become one of John's passions, and he was an ideal candidate to fill Marilyn's shoes. There was one concern that hadn't escaped our attention, however, and that was his health. John developed type one diabetes in his youth, and we knew that he frequently had episodes that required prompt attention. I had even placed a bottle of orange juice in the refrigerator at work for those times when his insulin levels were out of whack. We talked to him about his diabetes and he was confident that he could manage it and the presidency. After all, he had done just that at Merck-Medco.

At the September annual meeting (where I was barely functional), John was elected to his second two-year term. On the last Wednesday of November, the board was scheduled to meet and welcome me back. That morning, our administrative director Christina Memoli came sobbing into my office. She had just gotten off the phone with a friend of John's who called to inform us that John had died of a heart attack shortly after midnight. He had been at his summer home on the Cape wrapping up business for the board meeting. With his wife Emily still in Boston, he died alone. The heart attack was almost certainly a byproduct of the diabetes.

I was dumbstruck and wounded. How could this have happened? The absurd thought briefly passed through my mind that John had died in my place. I quickly banished this notion as rank egoism, and focused instead on what had to be done. I needed to call Barbara Roberts, our vice president. (She had in legal fact already become president at John's death.) She would have to chair the board meeting that evening. And then I would have to tell the faculty and staff, many of whom knew John from his role as a student, as well as for his governing functions.

What we couldn't do is call all the board members who would be present at the Music Center that evening. As they arrived, happy to see me, Barbara and I gave them the news. It was heartbreaking; it was shocking. Many couldn't fathom it at first, as I had felt on 9/11. Others like Leslie Colburn and Kurt Cerulli openly wept.

Barbara let everyone tell their personal stories about John. I would be lying if I said I remember all the accounts. The truth is that I just wanted the nightmare to go away. But as the evening drew toward its end, I was mindful that the cathartic storytelling not only helped us to manage our grief. It also reconfirmed everyone's commitment to the place that John loved so much. And Barbara, ever calm and steady, had begun to place her unique stamp on the position John occupied just seventeen hours before. She was already refashioning the presidency in her own image.

***

Soon my attention turned to producing a fitting memorial. Our neighbors at the Huntington Theatre Company proved cooperative, and we scheduled a remembrance at their new Calderwood Pavilion at the BCA. Sherrod Brown, John's best friend and an Ohio congressman about to be elected to the U.S. Senate, gave one of many moving tributes, as did his wife, the nationally syndicated columnist Connie Schultz. I represented the Music Center—one of too many occasions when I was called upon to eulogize a Music Center trustee.

That afternoon was a time for sharing tears and joy at having been part of John's life. But everyone also wanted a lasting memorial to celebrate the values that John brought to the Music Center. John was always highly supportive of our faculty members, and had made it his business to attend as many of their concerts as he could. The idea was to rename the Music Center's recital series, and the *John Kleshinski Concert Series* debuted the following year, headed with great skill and tact by pianist Stephen Yenger.

We also committed ourselves to an annual luncheon in John's memory at Hamersley's Bistro, one of America's premier restaurants. Gordon Hamersley was a member of the Music Center's corporation, and he quickly agreed to the idea. Each October for the next eight years until the Bistro closed in 2014, Gordon would host us on a sunny Sunday afternoon, serving his legendary roast children. The proceeds from the luncheon have helped establish a permanent endowment for the *John Kleshinski Concert Series*. The luncheon continued at Hamersley's former venue, Banyan Bar & Refuge, for two years, and in 2018, it was moved to City Winery Boston, a brand new space that attracted a whole new crowd, many of whom were hearing about John Kleshinski for the first time.

***

As 2006 drew to a close, I was more than happy to see the year go. I had survived pneumonia and two unexpected deaths. My friends had lent me more support than I could ever have hoped for. And I was already looking forward to my silver anniversary as executive director in 2008 and the Community Music Center of Boston's centennial in 2010. Important goals still laid ahead of me, and I was committed to working on them with renewed energy and dedication.

Chapter 42
Protégés

C. Thomas Brown began worshipping at the Church of the Advent in 1998 when he was still a Harvard undergraduate. Twenty-six years my junior, he sometimes reminded me of myself at that age—exceedingly smart and frequently haughty, but definitely more conservative in politics and art. He also intimidated me, probably because I found myself attracted to him. His dark features were not my usual cup of tea, but I had partaken of robust blends before, so he wasn't completely off the menu.

For reasons that remain elusive, we never really clicked until 2005 when a mutual love of opera began to nurture our budding relationship. We attended a memorable performance of *Rigoletto* that year in New York. A young Anna Netrebko was the hunchback jester's daughter Gilda and tenor Rolando Villazon impersonated the Duke of Mantua. Rigoletto himself was less impressive, but with Netrebko and Villazon on stage together, the sexual chemistry ran high—as did the level of charismatic singing.

We left the opera house on a high note, only to confront one of the worst blizzards to hit New York in years. O'Neal's Saloon was still open across Broadway so we retreated there for a bite to eat and to perform an operatic post mortem. But the staff was eager to close—understandably—and we left shortly for our respective Manhattan destinations. I took the subway to Penn Station, only to discover that all the trains in and out of the city had been halted. I called the Dimits who once again rode to my rescue, and offered to put me up for the night in their Chelsea residence. Through the years, I have crashed many times on the Dimits' sofa after an opera has ended, catching forty winks while awaiting a 2:40 AM departure back to Boston. In that way, I was able to arrive at work promptly and surprisingly well rested. Opera lovers are an intrepid breed!

Tom and I have worked together at the Advent. We are both acolytes and members of the Vestry—he is now senior warden. I also recruited him for the Music Center, where he has served on the corporation and finance committee. For a half-dozen years we have attended Boston Symphony performances together. At some point—I could not tell you when—I became more interested in Tom's exploits than pursuing my own with him (which were going nowhere in any event), and we settled into a long, rewarding and deep friendship. I consider him one of my closest allies, and little transpires in my life today that he isn't made aware of almost instantaneously.

At the Metropolitan Opera with Tom for Richard Wagner's Ring, 2019

***

"We gotta get Lapin out of here" was Mr. Brown's reaction to the multiple tributes lavished on me at my twenty-fifth anniversary gala in 2008. In fact, being an egomaniacal sort, I actually enjoyed every last one of them, especially the comments from Uncle Eddie who, with Aunt Dotty, had flown up from Florida for the occasion. I had taken them and cousin Lori for dinner at Hamersley's the night before, and Aunt Dotty especially was impressed that "everything was a la carte."

The gala was called *Quarter Note*, and it was held at the Calderwood Pavilion where we had saluted John Kleshinski two years prior. On this occasion, the Music Center orchestra was on hand to perform a Haydn symphony and a commissioned piece from the composer Eva Conley Kendrick. Months before the premiere, Eva asked me if I had a favorite poet whose words I might like set to music. I thought for a few seconds and said, "Anyone but Walt Whitman." Of course, I had placed my foot in my mouth, because Eva had already begun to compose a piece set to Whitman's free verse. I enjoyed it so much that I requested an encore for my thirtieth anniversary in 2013.

Quarter Note also marked the occasion for a proclamation making June 8, 2008 David Lapin Day in the City of Boston. In a statement read by Claudia Haydon and Lucy Sollogub, Mayor Thomas Menino cited me for exemplifying "a profound humanity and passion for inclusion, promoting access and diversity, nurturing youth, encouraging freedom of expression, and keeping the history, mission and spirit of Community Music Center of Boston's founders alive and of service to future generations." I was genuinely moved, especially because I so admired Mayor Menino's leadership and political savvy.

The event attracted an overflow crowd of several hundred well wishers, so many that the Calderwood staff had to place limits on the number of folks admitted to the post-concert reception. If all of this sounds like me tooting my own horn, I am. The occasion made me more aware than ever of how many lives I had touched, and I could not have been more thankful for the outpouring of affection on display that afternoon.

***

The event of which I am most proud is the annual David Lapin Competition for Music Center middle and high school students. We have always touted the day as a "friendly competition," and it is that, indeed. Many of the participants have grown up knowing and playing in ensembles with each other, and their mutual support is palpable. More than a few have gone on to appear with The Boston Pops under Keith Lockhart as part of Fidelity Investments' Young Artists Competition.

Each year, the Lapin Competition requires recruiting six noted musicians as judges (three for the juniors and three for the seniors). Their ranks have been drawn from the region's finest singers, instrumentalists and conductors. I hesitate to mention any for fear of leaving out the rest, but let me recognize those with special connections to the Music Center, including the late baritone Robert Honeysucker, who was our assistant director in the 1970s; the pianist and woman-composer champion Virginia Eskin, a past board vice president; and James Nicolson, also a former vice president, harpsichordist and teacher who joined our faculty in 1964. The composer Daniel Pinkham reminded me that he had been on the faculty in the 1940s. He especially loved the spicy meat patties brought to his solfege classes by a trio of Jamaican ladies. Recently, we brought back Kenneth Radnofsky, my former associate director and a one-man advocate for classical music for saxophone. If I've left out others, my apologies. I am grateful to all who have lent their names and talents over the past quarter century and more.

On my retirement in 2017, the Harold Whitworth Pierce Charitable Trust made a substantial grant to fund the Lapin Competition, as well as our Young Composers Festival. Lapin Competition contestants are my musical children, and I continue to observe their personal and professional growth with deeply-felt pride. The very first winner, Melissa Chow, is now past forty, and many participants like Dan Restuccia and Yangwei Situ have children of their own learning to play an instrument. It's possible that at some stage one or more of them will perform in the Lapin Competition, and a new tradition will be added to the many that distinguish Music Center history. I look forward to that day with keen enthusiasm.

Chapter 43
Gallows Humor

With *Quarter Note* behind me, I accepted an invitation from the New England Conservatory of Music to join a study group bound for Venezuela in June 2008. Music education has thrived in some of the most repressive political contexts (the composer Carl Orff prospered in Nazi Germany), and *El Sistema* is the latest exemplar of this phenomenon. Founded in 1975, the program has provided classical music instruction to impoverished Venezuelan youth as a catalyst for social change. *El Sistema's* musical success is unquestioned—hence our trip. Its social achievements are much less clear, as *El Sistema's* visionary founder, Jorge Abreu, had long since made his peace with his country's *jefe-presidente* Hugo Chavez.

Tony Woodcock, then president of the Conservatory, headed the delegation, which also included Linda Nathan from the Boston Arts Academy (the city's high school for the arts), Anita Walker from the Massachusetts Cultural Council, and other prominent arts leaders. I thought Tony brought a breath of fresh air to the Conservatory and to its connection to *El Sistema*. He was definitely no pushover, and he had trouble with the Conservatory making an open-ended commitment to train its Abreu Fellows to run "*nucleos,*" or *El Sistema*-inspired programs, in the United States. Others like Linda Nathan questioned *El Sistema's* focus on classical music and its suitability for American urban settings.

Whatever doubts were expressed, *El Sistema* had clearly provoked many of us to rethink our own pedagogy and operations. The four daily hours of after-school training and rehearsals that typify *El Sistema* programs in Venezuela were almost certainly not going to work in Boston. But its unique pairing in ensembles of older, more advanced students with young beginners was definitely something worth exploring. I had already given a seminar on arts administration to a cohort of Abreu Fellows at the Conservatory, and many of them would return to their own communities to start *El Sistema*-like programs. I was decidedly impressed by their enthusiasm, as I would be with the young musicians I observed in Caracas. The trip also provided the welcome occasion for a reunion with the mother of Patricia Espinosa, one of our best early childhood instructors. Patricia had primed me with a crash course on Venezuelan politics and culture before my departure.

In the past decade, *El Sistema* programs have sprouted across the United States. As they seek to adapt to local conditions, the line between *nucleos* and community schools of the arts continues to blur. And there's nothing wrong with that. What would be unfortunate is if the American infatuation with *El Sistema* turns out to be just another funding fad. I certainly hope that's not the case, because both *El Sistema* and community schools can learn and benefit from each other. There is ample opportunity for both to flourish, and the two models should be capable of producing rich musical dividends for many years to come.

***

Like oil profits in Venezuela, the prosperity of the American economy largely fuels support for new ventures like *El Sistema* USA, as well as long-established institutions like the Community Music Center of Boston. By October 2008, it became clearer by the day that we would be tightening our belts more than ever—at least during my tenure.

On a personal level, the Great Recession made me feel like a chump. I had scrimped and saved all my adult life, even denying myself a real bedroom until I was forty-two in order to keep my living costs as low as possible. And then, in a matter of months, almost half my savings were gone, poof. The American way of life didn't feel that promising or rewarding by the winter of 2008-09.

The Music Center hadn't fared any better. Giving in December 2008—usually the strongest month of the year—dried up. It was as if a water faucet had frozen. People were scared and with good reason. Financial markets had seized, and bedrock institutions like Lehman Brothers and Merrill Lynch disappeared or put themselves on the selling block. I recall a conversation at the time with the Music Center trustee Amy Merrill, granddaughter of the brokerage house founder Charles Merrill. Bank of America had to take over Merrill Lynch, and a firm that democratized financial markets for generations of Americans ceased to exist as an independent entity. Amy was devastated, and I could readily understand why. It was around this time that I discovered to my astonishment that Amy's babysitter, when she was a youngster, was none other than John Pearson, the man who introduced me to the Music Center in 1981.

With no end to the downward spiral in sight, I met with the Music Center's treasurer Kurt Cerulli. Kurt had founded a worldwide asset management and research analytics firm in

1992, headquartered in Boston's Back Bay. He didn't need me to tell him that things were tough. And yet, neither of us wanted to do what we knew in our guts had to be done—our staff and faculty had to take salary cuts. Leading by example, I trimmed my pay by 7.5 percent. All the senior staff sustained similar declines, and almost everyone else absorbed cuts of five percent or more.

Nothing tests institutional mettle like a good recession. To this day, I can only express my gratitude to all my employees who responded to their salary reductions with extraordinary grace. No one quit, and—most important—not one person was laid off. Several years later, we repaired the damage, restored pay rates, and even made an effort to compensate people for the losses they had sustained. I would not have thought such actions even remotely possible in 2009.

***

"You only have one opportunity to celebrate a centennial." With that note of gallows humor from Barbara Roberts, the Music Center went forward with plans for our hundredth anniversary in 2010. We intended to celebrate the milestone by producing one-hundred free concerts as a gift to the City of Boston. We also wanted to raise lots of money. Both goals had been placed in jeopardy by the prolonged financial crisis. We hired a well-regarded consultant to run a feasibility study for the proposed campaign. She had been recommended to us by our friends at City Hall, but her work proved uneven at best. Barbara has to be one of the easiest persons on Earth to get along with, but even Barbara found her off-putting. To make matters worse, she choked in her final recommendation, arguing that we should not attempt to raise any more money than we had a decade ago for our 90th Anniversary Campaign.

The neat thing about feasibility studies is you can tear them up and start afresh, which is just what we did. I didn't see any sense at all in establishing a target that duplicated what we had achieved in the previous decade. Yes, it would be tough, but I was determined to make the campaign work, recession or not. I felt like my reputation was on the line, and in committing to raising $3.5 million, it was.

Fortunately for the Music Center and me, the stock market hit rock bottom in March 2009, and then began a slow recovery. We weren't out of the woods by any means. But we had a fighting chance to reach our goal, and I wasn't about to let a once-in-a-hundred-year opportunity escape our grasp.

Chapter 44
A Centennial Celebration

The Music Center's centennial date was something of a moving target. Music lessons at South End House were given as early as 1908, but the newly-formed South End Music School's first executive committee meeting took place in 1910. Its sister school, The Boston Music School Settlement, also provided lessons in the North End in 1910, but it didn't incorporate until 1912. The truth is we had an array of dates and years to choose from, so we decided to celebrate the Centennial across two years, from September 2009 until September 2011. That gave us plenty of time, I thought, to produce a hundred concerts and raise three-and-a-half million dollars.

We then added a third element to the celebration—a three-month exhibition at the Boston Public Library at Copley Square detailing our history and describing our present citywide impact. The display featured memorabilia from our earliest years, as well as posters, invitations, and programs for special events going back decades. The dazzling visual presentation, which included videos, was the brainchild of two graphic design wizards, board member MB Flanders and our marketing director Justo Garcia. Our special events committee, which I once condescendingly labeled the ladies auxiliary guild, did a fantastic job in support of the overall effort, and the members produced an opening night gala that was truly stunning. Library officialdom was thrilled with our success, and they agreed to extend our stay by several months.

Over the life of the exhibition, we invited prospective lead donors for what we were calling The Centennial Campaign for Legacy & Innovation, chaired by Ropes & Gray attorney William Knowlton. One of the largest asks of the Campaign occurred over lunch at the Library with George Lewis, a cousin of The South End Music School founder Annie Endicott Nourse. George's cryptic response to my rather substantial request was that it would be "a big bump up." He then agreed to build a permanent endowment for our public school outreach efforts. Today, the George Lewis Fund continues to grow, and will support this program in perpetuity. Thank you, George.

***

We also met with donors off site, never more memorably than with Barbara Herzstein in Cambridge. Barbara and her husband Sigmund—Bud for short—had been introduced to me by the longtime chair of our corporation, H. Roderick Nordell. Rod had a knack for bringing rich donors into the Music Center orbit, and the Herzsteins more than capably filled that bill. When we originally conceived of the Centennial Campaign, I went to Bud and asked him for $250,000 to kickstart the drive. Bud was into business plans and strategic plans, and asked me to come back with a development plan for the Campaign. I took that as a very positive sign.

Some time passed, the plan was crafted, and I intended to share it with Bud, only to discover that he had died. Quiet man that he was in life, no news of his demise had filtered back to us. I thought our cause was lost when we didn't receive an expected year-end gift from his widow. And then, out of the blue, we heard from Barbara. Would our development director Claudia Haydon and I be able to visit her at her home on Fayerweather Street in Cambridge? Of course. We rehearsed our pitch, and I implored Claudia not to talk under any circumstances once we asked Barbara for the $250,000 and awaited her response.

Barbara welcomed us into her home, offered us sherry, and introduced her cat. After some twenty minutes, we dispensed with the small talk, and requested her gift. Barbara's back was to her widescreen television so she didn't see what Claudia and I had witnessed. The cat was crawling its way up the screen, leaving scratch marks in its wake. I could see the look of panic on Claudia's face, but true to her promise, she didn't say a word, giving Barbara time to consider the ask. Yes, she affirmed, Bud and she had agreed to the commitment before he died and "the money was there." Breathing a collective sigh of relief, Claudia and I thanked her and bade farewell. The cat also escaped at our departure, and I have no idea whether Barbara ever noticed the marks it had left on the television.

And then, Barbara died! Sad as we were at receiving this news, we were also stunned by our double dose of bad fortune. Both husband and wife had agreed to make a quarter-million dollar gift, and both had died before making it. Fortunately, Barbara had given us the name of her attorney to follow up on her pledge. Since we had nothing in writing, it took some persuasion before he agreed, but the happy news is we finally received the quarter million, and then some. Thank you, Barbara and Bud.

Words to the wise: persistence pays in the world of fundraising. And never let a crazy cat deflect you from keeping your eyes on the prize.

***

The Centennial years were my most exhilarating and time consuming since the move of 1990. It was going to be hard to come up with an encore, and by 2012, I must have started thinking about my plans to retire. Working at the Music Center had been energy depleting and life affirming. But it crowded out space for a personal life. Yes, I had the Advent, largely on Sundays. I had many friends, including those from the Music Center itself, but no "special someone," as the expression goes. I was okay with that, but I had to concede it was a tradeoff, nonetheless.

Travel continued to play a big role in my life, and in 2012 I visited Argentina and returned to *la douce* France for the first time since 1991. Argentina was a revelation, the only place I've ever been where you get counterfeit bills from a bank ATM that the same bank then refuses to accept because they're "*falso.*" I had a hard time with all the graffiti on private homes in Buenos Aires, but I got a chuckle over the discovery that more than half of Argentinians regularly visit psychologists. "It's the national pastime," opined Eunice Urcola—yet another Music Center expatriate who graciously showed me around town and beyond, especially sites along the beautiful *Rio Tigre*. I did enjoy my visit to *Recoleta* Cemetery, where Eva Perón is entombed, and a day trip to Uruguay's *Colonia del Sacramento*, a UNESCO-recognized maritime stronghold founded by the Portuguese in 1680.

France was wonderful as ever. I took Barbara Roberts's advice and hired a concierge from Paris Muse to guide me through the Louvre, which I had never previously visited. What a dope I was! I had an aversion to large museums and so had avoided it in the past—my loss, for certain. I also made my debut at the old Paris Opera at the *Palais Garnier*, where I saw a fine performance of Igor Stravinsky's *The Rake's Progress* in English with an American and Russian cast. So much for French culture.

***

The most amazing aspect to my France visit was that I got there at all. I left for JFK in New York on October 28 with a departure scheduled at 9:05 PM. It must have been the very last flight before Hurricane Sandy closed the airport—and much of New York City—for the next week. My return was equally charmed, as I landed at JFK with a connection to Boston just as the airport resumed normal activities. In all my years of travel I have rarely been inconvenienced by plane or train disruptions. Yes, there was that one time my sleeping car divorced from the rest of the *Lake Shore Limited* bound for Boston, and left us in an Ohio cornfield in the middle of the night. But even on that occasion, the train engineer took note of the separation, backed up the train, and recoupled us after only an hour's delay.

My principal reason for going to Paris in 2012 was to rendezvous with Edward Turk, who was giving a semester's film course at the Institute for Political Studies. Edward had sold me his interest in our Bay Village home the previous summer, but was still more or less living with me as a tenant in the subsequent months. All of that would change in 2013, as my domestic arrangement with the professor came to an end with his retirement from MIT and move to New York. And yes, our special friendship blossoms to this day—albeit without the Sturm und Drang that filled our lives for thirty-three years.

Chapter 45
Play Ball!

Baseball has been my on-again, off-again partner since I was five. Living in Bayside in 1956 I decided I was a Brooklyn Dodgers fan, but my heart belonged to the Yankees' Mickey Mantle, who had won the Triple Crown that year. Next year the Dodgers fled at the end of the season to Los Angeles and forfeited my allegiance, but I still remained a fan of the Mick. Actually, it wasn't until 1962 that I fell completely in love with number seven. When I was in bed with rheumatic fever, I watched or listened to every Yankees game except those with the Angels on the west coast where I probably fell asleep by the second or third inning. My heart collapsed when Mantle's foot got stuck on a chain-link fence in the Baltimore outfield that season, and it didn't revive until his return some thirty days later. Mantle went on to earn the MVP again that year, but his glory days were behind him. I still took his fan book to bed with me.

Another claim on my affections belonged to the southpaw pitcher Whitey Ford. Whitey's mother once worked at the A&P Supermarket next to Aunty Ann—or so I was told. It was enough for me to declare my allegiance to Whitey, who became my favorite pitcher until Sandy Koufax ousted him from my Pantheon around 1963. Years later, sanity prevailed, and I recognized the distinctive merits of both left handers. Kurt Cerulli, a baseball aficionado without rival, gave me an autographed baseball signed by Whitey, along with a signed portrait of Ford pitching in the 1962 World Series in San Francisco. I figured out he was pitching against the Giants in the photo only because the left-field foul pole indicated it was 335 feet from home plate, and Candlestick Park, then the home of the Giants, alone boasted that distance. Knowing facts like that is what makes baseball diehards as demented as opera fanatics.

In my teen years, I could not imagine rooting for anyone but the Yankees. Just to spite me, I suspect, my brother became a fan of the New York Mets, and his favorite player was a nondescript infielder named Al Moran. In my view, Jonny's baseball preferences were as inexplicable as his love for Bob Dylan and the Weavers. They just didn't align with my worldview. Why would anyone favor underdogs like the woebegone Mets? My commitment to the Yankees was purely based on their winning ways, because when they began their long slide toward mediocrity in 1965, my interests waned commensurately. They continued to lie dormant until Reggie Jackson, Mr. October, revived Yankee hearts and Nation in 1977.

***

I have sometimes been asked whether my love of baseball is connected with my sexual orientation. In plain-spoken terms, though it's never posed this bluntly, do I like baseball because I like guys? I guess my response is that I find the question mildly obnoxious. Still, there is a purity to the game that aligns in my mind with some ideal image of masculinity. Major-league Baseball also remains the exclusive provenance of males—at least, for now. I doubt that gay or straight guys respond to baseball differently. But the just-us-guys aura does have a certain appeal to it—and probably for some women, as well.

I have certainly been attracted to ballplayers. I think it would be unusual if I weren't. But typically that attraction is far more chaste than cynics would believe. In the 1990s the Red Sox third baseman was a good-looking guy named Tim Naehring. I definitely took note of his sex appeal, but I was just as drawn to him because we shared back problems, which in Naehring's case, contributed to his premature retirement. I worried about him and could empathize totally when his back forced him from games. I suppose you could say it was Mickey Mantle all over again, but with forty years of seasoning and hindsight.

***

Having been a lifelong switch hitter in so many ways, I found it relatively easy to dump the Yankees and cast my lot with the Red Sox. The decisive turn came in 1985, around the time that Roger Clemens burst on the scene. I had watched Red Sox games with mild interest since my move to Boston in 1980, and I enjoyed seeing the great Carl Yastrzemski in his final seasons. Still, it was Clemens and winning games that mattered and by 1986, I was hooked.

But the real lure of the Red Sox over the past quarter century hasn't been winning. Rather, it lies in rarely knowing how a game will turn out until the eighth or ninth inning. It's as if the Sox never give up and—for once in my baseball life—that never-say-die spirit trumped winning. Knuckleballer Tim Wakefield was the embodiment of that feeling, to which he added edge-of-your-seat anxiety. You just never knew when he was on the mound what would come next. Even for those who typically find baseball boring, watching Wakefield or sluggers like Manny Ramirez and David Ortiz—well, I could say a lot about them, but boring, never.

In 2004 Kurt Cerulli and I sat through the last game that season that the Red Sox would lose before going on to sweep eight straight and win their first World Series since 1918. The outlook was emphatically bleak, as was the weather. The temperature must have fallen below fifty, and by the bottom of the fifth, I felt the muscles in my rib cage shaking. Much of the depressed crowd had fled, and at some point we moved closer to the field. Maybe I thought it would be warmer there, but it wasn't. I wanted to leave so badly but I also wanted to stay. In the end it was a dispiriting loss. Kurt gave away his tickets for the next game, not knowing of course that the trajectory of Western Civilization itself would pivot the following evening.

***

That's baseball for you—tedious, winning, nail biting and exciting beyond all measure. In 2002 I traveled with Karen and Greg Dimit to Cooperstown, New York, home to opera's Glimmerglass Festival and baseball's hallowed Hall of Fame. We went to see both, but on this occasion I was especially eager to visit the latter. Karen Dimit remembered vaguely that her dad was a devoted fan of two brothers who played for the Pittsburgh Pirates. She couldn't recall their names—Paul and Lloyd Waner, AKA Big Poison and Little Poison—and Greg urged her to call her father for the information. She hesitated, maybe because she felt her father would think less of her for forgetting his heroes' names. Finally, she got up the gumption and phoned. Far from taking offense, he was profoundly moved that she had bothered to ask. We then visited the Waner plaques, and I could see a little mistiness in Karen's eyes. I think Greg and I intuited that this was a special moment for

The Education of Brainiac

Karen, and even Brainiac had a lump or two in his throat before we left the Hall of Fame that afternoon.

Karen Kettering Dimit and me outside the Baseball Hall of Fame, Cooperstown, New York

Chapter 46
Sight and Sound

Edward Turk's departure for New York in 2013 left me as a bachelor for the first time since my year in Ithaca in 1979-80. All of a sudden, I had three floors of Bay Village to myself. With the loss of Edward's share of our furniture, I decided to do something I'm rarely tempted to do: I went on a shopping spree. Not only did I buy a sectional sofa, a dining table and six chairs, a Persian rug, an Arts & Crafts chandelier, and lined curtains plus rods for my new bedroom. I also bought art—lots of art, representing New York to Boston to Provincetown artists. At some stage, Edward's Philip Cobb posed a question that must have been on a lot of folk's minds, "Where is he getting the money to buy all that stuff?"

In truth, I had always been cost conscious and rarely splurged on anything, aside from a couple of Ermenegildo Zegna suits. What I bought, I kept and maintained for years. I have purchased only two televisions my entire life and now I live without one. My Apple MacBook has lasted for twelve years, even though it chronically overheats. I've never bought a car. That saves tons of money. And so, I wasn't averse to buying more than I had been accustomed to, even if it meant putting a temporary dent in my savings account.

I started acquiring art in Provincetown, maybe around 2002. I was attracted to the abstract floral forms of the painter Jan Lhormer, who now teaches at Bridgewater State University, alongside my fellow Adventer Melanie McNaughton. I was drawn to the multimedia creations of my old friend Karen Kettering Dimit, a singer by training whose mosaics and sculptural forms especially sing to me. I also found the works of a few guys compelling. The New York-Provincetown artist Ted Chapin specializes in assemblage; he has managed to marry erector-set metalwork to the Biblical visuals of William Blake; I find that incredibly interesting. The P-town artist A. Paul Filiberto is well known, and I have two of his large canvases, both fairly abstract, of poppies and birch trees. And then there are the drawings and painted-vinyl videodiscs of Boston artist Mikey Carnes. Absolutely intricate and fascinating work. Mikey is also one of the best bartenders who ever poured me a drink—many, in fact.

All of these gifted individuals enrich my life. I never really thought I had much of a visual sense. My primary focus of course is aural. But over time I gained confidence in discerning what appeals to me visually, and what I want in my home. My mother always claimed that she was related to the *Art Nouveau* painter and illustrator, Théophile Alexandre Steinlen, whose *La tournée du Chat Noir* might be the most celebrated feline figure of all time. Who knows, maybe a fragment of Steinlen's DNA resides in me. In tribute to Mom, his art also adorns my walls and stairwells. I've also gotten Edward Feuerstein hooked on his works.

***

My harpsichord is most assuredly a work of art. Built in Montréal in 2016 by Yves Beaupré, it is a single-manual, bird-wing spinet fashioned after instruments of the late French

Baroque era. It is perfect for playing Couperin and Rameau, but I equally enjoy noodling over the English composers Byrd and Gibbons. Playing J.S. Bach is another matter. No one exposes weaknesses more cruelly than Johann Sebastian. There is no place to hide when playing Bach, all the more reason for me never to perform his music in public.

I have played to date in several recitals, as well as adult workshops. The latter are doubly fun because we get to drink wine once the ordeal ends. We adults are an altogether different species from our young colleagues. Our memory cells are usually shot to Hell, so we typically are spared from the agony of memorization. We also excuse ourselves a lot while playing, "I'm sorry, I'm sorry" being the most common pronouncement. That's a nasty habit, in my opinion, because more than half of the time, your audience doesn't even know you've made a mistake. But like all habits, it's difficult to jettison.

As I write this, two pieces compel my attention. The first is a deceptively simple Bach *Sarabande in b minor*. The second, by Couperin, is *Le dodo ou L'amour au Berceau,* which translates as *The Dodo, or Love in a Cradle*. Since the dodo was last heard in 1662 and Couperin was born in 1668, one can only imagine what inspired his riff on that bird. I think he must have had a cockeyed cuckoo in mind. There is a rocking quality to the music, so at least the cradle makes sense. My teacher Nickolai tells me I have a sixth sense in reaching for the correct keys without looking. Perhaps that helps with the rocking.

***

Early exposure to the arts has untold lasting effects on one's life, and mine is no exception. My early introduction to musical instruments was pivotal. But perhaps my most formative moment came in third grade when my visual arts teacher showed me a photograph of Georges Seurat's *A Sunday Afternoon on the Island of La Grande Jatte*. I cannot say why this particular nineteenth-century masterpiece had such an impact, but I immediately determined on my own with my teacher's help to recreate the painting as a construction paper mosaic. I loved the act of assembling the images, of bringing some unity and order out of the little, disparate pieces of paper.

Perhaps not surprisingly, I wasn't really satisfied with the result—it seemed so inadequate to my aspiration! This perfectionist impulse has been my Achilles' heel all my life. I now realize that, even if I was a trifle hard on myself for not having produced a second masterpiece worthy of Seurat, I took great pleasure in the act of creating my mosaic.

Of course, I did not realize at the time how privileged and fortunate I was to go to a private school that could afford to hire an art teacher for third graders. As I look back today, I recognize that my lifetime of work at the Community Music Center of Boston has been a form of payback to all my music and art teachers. My vocation itself—a calling, if you will—was also nothing less than the fulfillment of a third-grader's dream to be involved in the arts.

At my last National Guild conference as the Music Center's executive director, in 2016, I paid a visit to the Art Institute of Chicago with one goal in mind. I went right up to *La Grande Jatte* and thanked Monsieur Seurat for all the blessings he has sent my way. He will always have *mon remerciement*.

The Education of Brainiac

At *La Grande Jatte*

Chapter 47
Succession

Planning my retirement gala was like producing my own funeral. It required tact, sensitivity, thoughtfulness and attention to detail. It meant preparing an invitation list, choosing the music to play and who would perform it, deciding on eulogists and how many, and, above all, determining what I would wear. I didn't have to pick out a casket, but then again neither I nor anyone else will be doing that when I truly bite the dust.

Anyway, I'm getting ahead of myself. The first formal step toward retirement was to organize a board retreat. For someone who trumpeted the virtues of institutions all his adult life, the truth is I had run the Music Center pretty much on the fly—not much differently than how the organist and doctor Albert Schweitzer operated his makeshift hospital in Lambaréné, Gabon. I was loathe to write down or enforce rules and regulations. I thought it would crimp my style and set boundaries that I might want to ignore. We didn't have a strategic plan until John Kleshinski's presidency, and the same went for an employee handbook. My relationships with staff members were largely informal and personal. I tried to be fair and evenhanded, yet there was scant written documentation to judge objectively how fair or equitable my treatment of individual employees was. I liked that.

All of this would have to change in a period of transition, and this is how the theme of institutionalization came to dominate the board retreat of January 2016, as well as the next eighteen months. The board itself had been effectively served by Kurt Cerulli, who had succeeded Barbara Roberts as president in 2010. One of my biggest blunders as executive director had occurred early that year when I failed to discern that Kurt was receptive to moving from treasurer to president. I think he felt hurt that he was wasn't initially offered the post, and only Barbara Roberts' intense diplomatic skill saved us from my faux pas. Beverly Arsem, Barbara's vice president—and the architect who oversaw the renovation of my home in 2003—was incredibly gracious in removing her name from contention, and Kurt was elected by acclamation at the September 2010 annual meeting.

***

Kurt's time as president coincided with the successful completion of our Centennial celebrations and the Campaign for Legacy & Innovation. He and his wife Mary had been among the top donors to that effort. We were all at the top of our game, and that is often a dangerous place to be. On the heels of her success as development director, Claudia Haydon resigned. Kimberly Khare would leave her post as head of music therapy, and our registrar Andy Mahoney followed suit. The paucity of resignations from the faculty during the Great Recession produced a cascading effect in succeeding years.

Fortunately, much of the senior staff remained unchanged. Will Fickes was still associate director and Lucy Sollogub continued to head school outreach. But even this stability provoked angst among grantmakers who were concerned about our lack of a succession plan for Will, Lucy and me. Only Marie Tai, our administrative director (and someone who literally had grown up at the Music Center), was far from retirement.

All these issues were productively addressed at the retreat, and a blueprint was drawn up to begin an elaborate strategic planning process—overly elaborate, in my estimation. The consultant who led the retreat did a bang-up job, and we hired her to lead the planning process as well. Everyone loved her at the retreat. Not everyone loved her over the next six months. I don't think it was her fault. The chemistry of relationships changes over time and what worked on a full tank in January just ran out of gas by June.

There is exactly one consultant in my professional life whom I have respected and gotten along with over the long haul. Development counsel Susan Galler calls herself a professional nag. She is certainly that, and more. She ran retreats for us, capital campaigns, executive coachings; the only thing we haven't asked of her is to run a job search. I forget how she came to the Music Center, but whoever suggested her deserves extra credit. Every December, Susan sends me a package of what were once called Mystic Mints. They're chocolate-covered Oreos and one of my gustatory guilty pleasures. Susan may know how to stay on my good side, but the plain truth is she'd be there tomorrow and beyond even without the Oreos.

***

The Carney and Nicholls families were Music Center legends from the sixties forward. Over time, each boasted eleven or more siblings studying everything from violin to clarinet to guitar. The Nicholls family's involvement at the Music Center was profiled in *The Christian Science Monitor* in the seventies in an article by Rod Nordell. The Carneys were just as intrinsic if less renowned. The Nichollses were from the Caribbean and the Carneys were pure Irish.

In the nineties, both clans were represented on the board of directors. When we were designing a commemorative booklet for the school's ninetieth anniversary, a photo from the sixties struck a resonant chord in me because one of the children in the picture looked just like our then-current student, John Carney. I asked John's mother Mary if she could identify the child, and she confirmed it was none other than her husband Barney at age twelve. Both father and son resembled each other, but the clincher for me was that Barney held his hands in his pockets in the exact same manner as his son John forty years later. I wonder if there is a gene for that.

It was not especially uncommon for husbands and wives to serve on the board either simultaneously or in staggered terms. Greg and Karen Dimit had done so, as had Eric and Hilary Wodlinger, and George Hein and Emily Romney. (George was the very first person I asked to join the board, in 1983.) Some years after Barney's service ended, Mary Carney was recruited for board service, and at the time of the Centennial, she had served as Kurt Cerulli's vice president. There is no expectation that vice presidents will move up to the presidency and, Barbara Roberts aside, it remains a rare occurrence. Still, Mary seemed ideally poised to fill Kurt's shoes, and in September 2014, she became the last of my ten presidents.

I wasn't sure if I'd get along with her at first, though I had known her for many years. Unlike Kurt, she talked a lot, which always gets on my nerves. She questioned long-established practices, and that really annoyed me. But she also had a knack for engaging board, faculty and staff in conversation. She was exquisitely sensitive to my ego's needs as I contemplated retirement. And she was amazingly adept at putting out all the little brush fires that inevitably ignited as people began to adjust to the prospect of a post-Brainiac era.

Edward Feuerstein accompanied me to Chicago in 2016 for the National Guild conference, where I was to be recognized for my longtime involvement in the Guild and the Music Center. He met Mary and somehow the subject turned to fruitcakes, as we were only a few weeks from Christmas. Now, Edward makes a really unusual, yeastless fruitcake. Mary feigned interest in Edward's fruitcake, and the following month she was awarded a sample of the holiday season delicacy. That's the kind of president Mary was, sacrificing her palate to please my best friend. If "No good deed goes unpunished" were personified, her name would be Mary Carney.

Chapter 48
Arts on the Rise

The Harvard Musical Association could only exist in Boston. Founded in 1837 principally to promote music studies at Harvard (there were none at the time), the Association has been independent of the University for almost its entire history. Its primary mission today is to produce chamber music concerts for members and their guests. String quartets are especially prized, though the first performance I attended twenty years ago featured a solo program by the pianist Peter Serkin.

I had reservations about joining HMA after my first visit. By and large, the members appeared quite creaky. Whether because of advanced age or the absence of tags, many couldn't recall the names of fellow members they had known for years, if not decades. Everything about the place reeked of stuffiness, and in the case of the atmosphere literally so. After each concert, members usually retire upstairs for a repast of Welsh rarebit and baked beans. I've often wondered how musicians don't pass out smelling the beans baking during their performances.

HMA also does good works on a modest basis. Not long after I joined, Judith Strang-Waldau asked me to participate in the high school achievement awards committee. I had known

Judith for some time as she worked first at the Neighborhood Music School in New Haven and then the Rivers Music School outside Boston. Judith was cool, and utterly atypical for an HMA member. Working with her would be a pleasure, so I agreed. We served together for about fifteen years and many of our earliest high school musicians are now professional players. She stepped down last year as chair of the committee and I succeeded her in that capacity. My fellow committee members are all wonderful musicians. Two of them, violists Michael Loo and Marcus Thompson, actually preceded me as members. The violinist Irina Muresanu and pianist Bonnie Guy Donham came on board several years ago. Our latest addition, soprano Letitia Stevens, is a friend from the Church of the Advent, where she sings in the professional choir.

Judith Strang-Waldau, in buttons, with me

The high school achievement awards competition attracts applicants from among Massachusetts' finest young musicians. A group of finalists are invited each year to perform for us, and awards are then made to the top three performers. This year's results were unusual because two pianists tied for first place;

their performance styles were so different that we couldn't possibly rank one over the other. I may be biased as chair of the committee, but I actually think that the finals concert is among the most important on HMA's annual calendar. Without these youngsters and others like them, there will be no HMA in the future—or classical music, for that matter. We need to do all we can to nurture young talents, not simply because they will become tomorrow's top performers. They will also help create future discerning audiences for their music. They extend HMA's and classical music's DNA, and toward that end I remain committed body and soul.

***

Another organization where I hope to make a difference is EdVestors, whose mission is to improve Boston Public Schools' capacity to deliver dramatically improved student outcomes. One of its long-standing interests is arts education, and the Community Music Center of Boston has profited enormously from EdVestors' strategic philanthropy—as have the many public schools with which the Music Center partners. I now sit on EdVestors' arts expansion advisory board.

In 2016 the Music Center produced the first of two galas in honor of my retirement. The evening was called *Crescendo: Arts on the Rise*—a Bourbon cocktail dubbed the *Lapin Legato* from Mad River Distillers made its debut at the opening reception—and the keynote speaker was EdVestors' founder and CEO Laura Perille. Laura spoke eloquently about Boston's two-pronged effort to improve public school arts instruction by hiring over one-hundred new music and art teachers since 2007 and deepening relationships with external partners like the Music Center. This upbeat message often gets lost in the media, which seems more comfortable with the old meme detailing public school decline. In fact, Boston public schools are in far better shape today than when I arrived at the Music Center in 1981. And the improvement in arts instruction is a model for urban systems across the United States.

How did this happen? A lot of hard work on the part of many people including two effective mayors, a couple of good school superintendents among others not so good and, above all, a spirit of can-do cooperation fostered by the likes of Laura Perille. In 2018 Mayor Walsh asked Laura to serve as interim superintendent for the Boston Public Schools. More power to her.

***

Brent Parrish hit the ground running when we hired him to replace Claudia Haydon as development director. Brent exudes high energy and isn't shy about voicing strongly-held opinions. I liked that, others did not, and he quickly became the Music Center's disruptor, both as a positive force for change while hitting resistance with pushback from colleagues and board members. I facilitated more than a few mediations between him and our marketing director Catherine Miller, also no wall flower. Much of the tensions between them arose from the usual frictions that marketing and development generate in any institution. But their problems were also due to personality clashes. Both really did their jobs extremely well, and I was happy with each, but the stress of having to handle their squabbles—and others to be truthful—definitely contributed to my decision to retire. I no longer had the patience I once had to manage employees, especially those less than half my age. I wanted out, and I knew the time had come to let people know.

At the September 2015 annual meeting of the faculty, I signaled my intention to leave on August 31, 2017. Some board and staff members had known prior to that, so I felt I had given everyone fair warning. In retrospect, I wouldn't have done anything differently. The board became empowered as never before to shape the Music Center's future, and in that process, I could already feel my authority beginning to slip away. There's nothing wrong with that; I just had to resign myself to the inevitable and make my exit as gracefully as possible.

Chapter 49

Crescendo

I originally wanted my leave taking to be via balloon, like the Wizard of Oz. But the permitting process would have been daunting, so I settled for a black tie affair at the Cyclorama, where I had worked for twenty-seven years. Mary Carney and I initially thought about staging the gala at the John F. Kennedy Presidential Library, which boasts an expansive view of Boston Harbor—weather permitting. The Edward M. Kennedy Institute had just opened next door, and we also considered that venue, mainly because I hosted Ted Kennedy and actress Jane Alexander during their mid-nineties tour of Massachusetts mobilizing support for the National Endowment for the Arts. Ironically, that event was also produced at the Cyclorama, and in the end, we decided to stage my apotheosis on our familiar home turf. The date we agreed upon was September 16, 2017.

Senator Kennedy and wife Vicki, circa 1993. The young musicians are Marilyn Morrissey's son, Glen Ryan, and Mary Carney's daughter, Andrea Carney.

Anyone who's rented the Cyclorama rotunda knows it's a bare-boned house. Almost everything needs to be imported. The plus side is that you can let your creativity run wild—especially if money is no object. Fortunately, we approved a generous budget for the evening. My impending retirement was cause for my fourth and final capital campaign, headed by business reengineering guru James Champy, a former Music Center parent. Brent and I had already secured a two-year commitment from Bloomberg Philanthropies and their consultant had recommended the drive—the thought being that many would want to give in my honor—and donors did, liberally, in seven figures.

***

I had hoped early in the planning process that everyone who wanted to attend the gala could. But as that proved impractical, we decided to stage a free, al fresco event on June 17 called Lapin *Fête de la Musique*. Modeled after the French celebration of the summer solstice, the *Fête* had become an annual Music Center event in 2014. It was already a highly popular tradition—we staged it in various South End parks with live entertainment—and for the Lapin *Fête* we also closed down Warren Avenue and threw a street fair right outside the Music Center. About a thousand people showed up, including alumni from the eighties forward.

Of course, the morning of the event, I threw my back out. It got worse as the afternoon progressed. Riding an elephant didn't help—it was fake, but that didn't comfort my back. By the end of the day, I was ready for bed and I recovered fully only in time for my annual August trip to Provincetown.

I tried to tell myself that June's Lapin *Fête* and September's *Crescendo* (we recycled the title from the prior year) weren't about me. That was a trick that Father Cranston had taught acolytes twenty years prior. It works to a degree. Still, I was terribly anxious even though I had learned from decades of practice to hide my real emotions. As is my habit, I wrote a speech for *Crescendo* and practiced delivering it over and over so that it would sound utterly smooth, if not spontaneous.

There were three hundred patrons present on September 16 and I wish I could say I knew every one of them. In fact, I was amazed at the number of people I had never met before. I took that as a positive sign for the Music Center, as fresh faces would be needed for the new era that officially began on September 1 when Lecolion Washington became executive director.

Crescendo also served to introduce Lecolion to the broader public. I delivered a few gifts to him, including a fancy plunger to assist with our still-chronic plumbing woes and a giant flyswatter made from a photo of my face. That probably got the biggest laugh of the evening—or maybe it was my deadpan delivery modeled after Senate Majority Leader Mitch McConnell. Either way, I delivered the goods.

Of course, there was a heavy dose of nostalgia also. Eva Conley Kendrick composed a new piece for the occasion, "The Journey," much as she had done for Quarter Note in 2008. Stephen Yenger introduced a Community Music Center of Boston anthem. There were video testimonials from Robert Nicholls, representing the Nicholls siblings, former board presidents, staff and faculty members, parents, and Boston Pops maestro Keith Lockhart, speaking on behalf of the city's music community.

Aunt Dotty flew up from Florida—Uncle Eddie had recently passed away—just after Irma wreaked its damage on the Hurricane State. Ditto for Michael Parola, a percussionist on our faculty in the 1980s and 1990s, and one of the closest friends I made among our teachers past and present. Michael was reunited with his former pupil Charles "Sticks" Lingos, a music therapy student since 1978. My brother, Little Jonny, also lived in Florida by now, but multiple maladies made his presence impossible. My cousin Lori drove up from New York. Among other faculty members in attendance, I have bonded most closely with guitarist Javier Rosario—a soulmate and honorary *esposo* to whom I needn't explain anything about myself that he doesn't know already.

The Church of the Advent had two tables, headed by Tom Brown and Father Warren. Part of that crowd spilled over to the Beacon Hill table—the theme of the evening focused on Boston neighborhoods that the Music Center serves. Melissa Zeller attended, the woman who taught me to project enthusiasm at all times. Melissa shares my appreciation for Jeanette MacDonald, and I once gave her a handkerchief of Jeanette's that I had won at a Clan Clave raffle. There were so many former and current Board members that I dare not mention their names for fear of leaving someone out. Joan Nordell, our beloved Rod's widow, arrived on the arms of her son John, who had photographed my first fundraiser—the Bach Birthday Bash—in 1984. Board presidents from Ginger Lawrence forward were on hand, along with Hilary Wodlinger, Eric's wife. Boston Latin School and Berklee College of Music had their own tables, the latter headed by my longtime colleague Curtis Warner.

Bay Villagers came in flocks, shepherded by Leslie J. Colburn—whom I have known practically since moving to Boston—alongside the Village's *doyenne extraordinaire*, Jo Campbell. Jo was friends with my original landlords and knows everyone's story, for better or for worse. My National Guild buddies Eric Bachrach, Calvin Herst, Susan Randazzo and Lawrence Zukof especially honored me by their presence. And Andrea Kaiser, who has been a presence at the Music Center in multiple guises for over fifty years, also sponsored a table.

At my table were Aunt Dotty, Cousin Lori, Greg and Karen Dimit, the two Edwards, Philip Cobb, Philip and Edward Turk's friend Barry Macmillan, and Gordon Hamersley—a dyed-in-the-wool Red Sox fan. Later that month, Gordon emailed to tell me what a nice time he had. I replied to say that when the history of the Boston Center for the Arts is written, it should note that he and I had first and third covered. I regretted not inviting young Austin Rowe, my personal trainer, even though I had only met him that month.

***

I ended my speech with the same message contained in my Yale application forty-six years before. "It's only the very few saints among us who consistently do good in the absence of institutions that bind us together, mediate our differences, and propel us toward a common cause.

"I know as you do that most of our mainstream institutions in America are under siege—from government to business to religion to education. Many have failed us badly. But that's all the more reason to commit ourselves to their renewal. On our own small turf, I can leave the Music Center and you this evening secure in the knowledge that we—through this institution—have helped bind Bostonians together. It was true in 1910. It was true in 1981 when I arrived. It is true today.

"But my friends, it doesn't just happen. The Community Music Center of Boston will only prosper when we commit ourselves to its mission by working together beyond our day-to-day concerns and toward its larger purpose.

"Yes, the Music Center has given me a good life. For that I am deeply grateful to all of you and to those who came before you. I know, too, that with your support and with sleeves rolled up, it will continue to do magic for many, many years to come."

And with that, Brainiac turned over a new page in his ever-evolving life.

Chapter 50

Afterglow

Labor Day weekend 2017 found me briefly out of sorts. I should be working, I thought, but then—even had I not just retired—I wouldn't be working on Labor Day. It took me about four days to adjust to my newfound freedom, and by Wednesday, I was ready to move on. My reaction was much the same as to the loss of relationships and loved ones. I recover too fast, I don't know why, but sentimental attachment simply isn't in my makeup.

Maybe, too, I'm just hedging my bets. I've always had an inner circle of close friends, but—four or five aside—the members keep rotating. Edward Feuerstein rightly identifies my penchant for making younger friends, even as I myself get older. At the Advent, Stephen, Lynda, Julianne and Carolyn have been good friends for decades, but most of my Advent friends are one or even two generations behind me. I befriended Tom, Dustin, Nick, the two Michaels, Eric and Melanie when they were in their twenties. I'm certain there will be others joining the list in years to come.

Austin Rowe was twenty two when we met. Part of my post-Music Center plan was to resume activities I had jettisoned in the eighties. Joining a gym was at the top of the list. I liked Equinox Sports Club because it has a pool, and despite the premium cost, I signed up right after Labor Day. I also thought that since I had been out of action for so long, I should work with a personal trainer. Little did I realize where that would lead.

My first session was part-interview, part-workout. Austin wanted to know if I had any goals. I made them up. I said I wanted to lose weight and gain muscle—what else was I gonna say? He then walked me to a bicycle with a flywheel, which I mounted and rode for about five eternal minutes. By the end of our meeting, I was exhausted. And yet, while walking home, endorphins must have kicked in because I felt truly exhilarated. Getting back to structured physical activity—my teenage bugaboo—was going to be fun. And working with Austin would be its own reward.

That October, I left for the Pacific Northwest, courtesy of EdVestors, which had run a raffle for its donors, first prize being two JetBlue tickets to anywhere in the United States. I won and took Edward Feuerstein along to visit a bunch of friends from my Yale days, including Wally Jaffe and Paul King in Portland, John Treat and Doug Lind in Seattle, and Louis Allaire, my first Elm Street housemate, in Vancouver. We had a great time in all three cities, and I especially enjoyed visiting the Seattle Chihuly Garden and Glass Exhibit for the first time.

On my return, I resumed a twice weekly regimen with Austin. Personal training had come a long way since the eighties, and I was amazed by his overall skill and sixth sense for knowing just how far to push me. By Thanksgiving, Edward Turk noticed that my face was thinner. I was beginning to lose weight, which was terrific. Adding muscle proved to be more challenging. By Christmas the weight loss was noticeable to everyone. I rewarded Austin with a pair of duck socks—just the kind that

Catherine Miller gave me for my first and last duck boat tour, yet another event tied to my retirement. Twenty-five pounds evaporated in under four months.

We were having a great time in our sessions. After New Year's, I bumped up our frequency to three times a week. By then, he was calling me Dashing David and I labeled him Awesome Austin. I also compiled a list of adjectives to go with his initials AR. I should say that I had no idea where all of this was heading, nor did I have a clue where I wanted it to go, if anywhere. I did know that I was headed to Florida for a month and needed someone to water my harpsichord, as Austin phrased it. (Meaning—adding water to the humidifier.) I gave him my keys as he had agreed to be the "water boy," and I departed for South Beach.

I had a great time in Florida and enjoyed intimate relations while there with two folks of different genders—I don't think "both" is correct anymore. That was something I hadn't done in ages. The Edwards were aghast, but so be it. Then, one day, I got an email from a Music Center trustee, Ted Pietras. "I met ur tenant/roommate in the sauna room at club. I gather he's a trainer there. Small world." Whoa, that was news, indeed. I had told Austin somewhat ambiguously that I just didn't see the point of his staying in North Quincy once his lease was up. I guess he took that as an open invitation, which was fine with me, and on my return to Boston at vacation's end, I had a new roommate for the first time since 2013.

Awesome Austin with his Christmas present from me

The next six months went by swiftly. Austin really wanted to open his own gym, and though we looked all over Boston for spaces, the high rentals made it completely infeasible. By late July, I knew he would head to Denver, where he'd pair up with another Equinox trainer and start their own facility. I also knew that leaving was best for both of us. We had a terrific year together, but it was time once again to move on.

***

Today I have a great trainer named Pete Goulet. His mantra is "Think cow"— as distinct from "Think cat"—a contrast which helps me with my training and spinal alignment at least as much as "Think Mick Jagger" helped me to snorkel at the Great Barrier Reef. He's also a terrific guy, and we banter a lot during our sessions. I'm still playing harpsichord, thanks to my ever patient teacher Nickolai. My calendar is replete with meetings for the Massachusetts Turnpike, EdVestors, Harvard Musical Association and, above all, the Church of the Advent.

As I finish this chapter, we are past Palm Sunday and reliving what Christians experience as the Passion of our Lord and

Savior Jesus Christ. It is the holiest week of the Christian calendar, and I approach it with mindfulness of my duty to proclaim the Good News that Easter brings to all who open their hearts and souls to it. If anything in the preceding pages strikes you as conflicting with that obligation, banish the thought from your mind. Life's disparate threads are all connected, and I am happy to have shared mine with you.

Mrs. Stabile's Spaghetti Sauce and Meat Ball Recipe From Frieda, July 12, 1982

...As for the spaghetti sauce, I don't know if I can give you the exact amounts—I only learned how to make it by watching Mrs. Stabile's mother-in-law when she made it. Of course, she didn't tell me the amounts of ingredients (she never spoke English) so I will try my best to give you some idea as best I can.

1 6 oz. can tomato paste preferably imported
1 8 oz. can tomato puree or sauce
1 c. water
1 tsp. sugar – a few dashes of salt and pepper
1 tablespoon dried basil (or if you can get fresh, use about 2 leaves)

In heavy saucepan, pour enough olive oil to cover bottom of pan. On medium heat, brown the chopped onions [note she neglected to include this above] until just golden (not too dark or burned). Add the paste & sauce & water, stir together thoroughly—then add the remaining ingredients, mixing well. Here is where you again use your own judgement [sic]. If it seems a bit too thick at this time, gradually add a bit more water (about ½ c.). Bring sauce to a boil then lower heat on simmer for at least an hour. (The "natives" used to do this for 3 or 4 hrs.)

P.S. I meant to tell you – if you want the sauce with the accompanying meatballs, sausage or whatever, you must brown these items slightly, before adding to sauce.

Italian meatballs:

1 lb. chopped beef or a mixture of beef, pork & veal
1 egg — 1 tbsp. chopped parsley
1 tsp. garlic powder
1 tbsp. grated Romano cheese
½ c. breadcrumbs

Mix all ingredients together thoroughly. Again, if mixture is a bit too wet, add additional breadcrumbs a little bit at a time. Roll the meatballs in about 1" size. Brown lightly. Add to sauce. Note—add the pan droppings to sauce—don't discard.

I hope you understand this all. Maybe you should type this up so you can have it handier to read. Well, that's about it, hon. Let me know how it all turns out for you.

Love,
Mom

Acknowledgments

A memoir is by its nature an accounting of recollections, and I have tried to remain as true to my memories as humanly possible. That doesn't mean that the facts will always align with the memories, and I thank all the individuals who helped me to correct errors of fact. In rare instances I have toyed with facts in order to preserve a narrative arc or to obscure a person's identity. When a name is introduced for the first time in quotation marks, it indicates that the character may be a composite of more than one figure, or I may simply not recall the person's name. On the fiction-fact spectrum, consider that character a tad closer to the former.

I wish to thank all the persons mentioned throughout *Brainiac* who had enough confidence in me to give their express permission to use their names without knowing what I had to say about them. They helped make the publisher's onerous requirement an easier chore to complete than I would have expected. To those who requested a sneak preview before granting permission, recall that Saint Thomas remained an apostle in good standing—despite his doubts! For the record, only two persons requested that their names be left out of Brainiac's story, and I have honored that request.

This process also gave me an occasion to get in touch with some folks whom I hadn't seen or talked to in over fifty years.

It has been a great pleasure to renew these acquaintances. I especially thank Edward Baron Turk and Edward Feuerstein for contributing the Foreword and Interlude, respectively. Both also read the manuscript in various stages, and offered helpful suggestions, as did Dustin Henderson. Stephen J. Morgan and Emily Paul also lent their enthusiastic assistance.

Finally, I should thank Amtrak, for its *Silver Meteor*, and Apple, for its iPad. Both technologies conspired to make *The Education of Brainiac* possible.

About the Author

Born in New York City and raised in Puerto Rico and Queens, New York, David Lapin led Community Music Center of Boston, one of the nation's largest and oldest community schools of the arts, from 1983 until 2017. In that capacity, he served on the boards of the Boston Annenberg Challenge, the Boston Center for the Arts, the National Guild for Community Arts Education, and numerous city task forces on arts education. He is a past president of the National Guild, a former member of the Walnut Hill School for the Arts Board of Visitors and the school quality review team for Boston Arts Academy, the city's high school for the arts. A member of the Harvard Musical Association (HMA), Lapin holds a Ph.D. in political science from Yale University, and has taught at Yale and Cornell.

Lapin has also served on many diverse panels for HMA, Berklee College of Music, Longy School of Music of Bard College, the Massachusetts Cultural Council and the New England Conservatory. He has been an advisor to The Learning Project in Boston's Back Bay and Jamaica Plain's Eliot School of Fine Arts. He continues to serve on the advisory board for EdVestors Arts Education Fund and the Vestry of Beacon Hill's historic Church of the Advent, where he chairs the Administration Committee. He also chairs HMA's Achievement Awards Committee.